FEARLESS BEAUTY

MIKEY MORAN

FEARLESS

BEAUTY

THE HAIR BUSINESS
BLUEPRINT

LIONCREST
PUBLISHING

FEARLESS BEAUTY

The Hair Business Blueprint

ISBN   978-1-5445-2008-7 *Hardcover*
           978-1-5445-2007-0 *Paperback*
           978-1-5445-2006-3 *Ebook*

Hey, Mom! I know you are watching from above. This one's for you.

CONTENTS

INTRODUCTION

One sale a week can change your life. A sale a day can pay your rent.

I know because I've lived it.

My childhood wasn't too tough compared to some—I was never abused or homeless—but it was always a struggle. We lived, balanced on that razor's edge between okay and not making it. And by "balanced," I mean wobbled, tiptoed, and pin-wheeled.

I also had a couple of undiagnosed learning disabilities. If I were coming up through the school system today, someone would probably have figured it out, but at the time, I just knew learning and getting stuff done was harder for me than it was for "normal" people. My mom was a single parent living with her mom, and they were both very school-focused. They thought education was going to be the way I could make a better life for myself. I tried, but I never did too well in school. I didn't understand how to learn properly. The right school for me wasn't school. It was starting a business.

I started working at fourteen, knocking on neighborhood doors with a snow shovel, rake, or mower depending on the season. Wanting to take away Mom's financial anxieties motivated me to start my first business and then my second when the first went over the edge.

It took me ten years to find my idea—CurrySimple. I loved Thai food and did a ton of research and created an authentic prepared curry sauce. People loved it, but I was trying to do it all on my own without enough money and no experience or coaching. It was a big idea full of failure, but it was the perfect education. It taught me the way I needed to learn. But it was like learning about gravity by jumping off a house rather than believing what the science books have to say.

After CurrySimple failed, I tried to start a few other small businesses, but nothing really caught on. I got into hair when a friend of mine mentioned his girlfriend spent over three grand a year on hers. I didn't know anything about it, but I'd learned enough about how to start and run a business that I was ready to make this one work. I hadn't gone to business school, but I had a PhD from the university of failure and I'd learned everything I needed to know—everything I've now put into this book. Private Label Extensions went from nothing, with no outside investment, to placing 278th on the Inc. 500, to being named one of the fastest-growing beauty companies in America. And if I sound proud of that, it's because I am.

In the five years since, I've helped thousands of women build their own companies. Most of them are a lot like I was starting out—they've got something they want to change. They're passionate and more than ready to work hard at turning what they love into a career or side hustle.

Most of the women I've worked with start out with a couple of advantages I didn't have. Many have been stylists who wanted to start selling hair extensions or wigs out of their salons. Some had other careers in the beauty business, and others were just obsessed with it. But they all had a long-standing interest in beauty and were already knowledgeable about hair. They had experience I didn't, but like me when I launched CurrySimple, they had no idea where to start. Also, many had the entrepreneur's personality but, like I did, lacked the core skills of entrepreneurship. Luckily for them, I'd already made about every mistake you can make in the hair business, and it had taught me how not just to think but to act like an entrepreneur.

I've put all that—everything I wish I'd known or done, everything I've learned from my own experience and from helping others—into this book to help you get from wherever you are to that first sale. And from there to one sale each week, to one a day, to one (or more) every hour. To give you an idea of the possibilities—during the writing of this book, Private Label Extensions sold $113,000 in twenty-four hours. Talk about life-changing!

But to get to life-changing, you've got to change your life.

I'm not talking about changing who you are. If you've read this far, there must be something big you want to do. That entrepreneurial hunger is the one thing you've got to have to start your own business, and it's something no one can teach you (in fact, I'll bet someone's tried to teach it out of you), but it isn't all you need. To get from where you are to that first sale, to become an entrepreneur and build your own hair business, you need two things—you need to be fearless, and you need a blueprint.

I can't make you fearless, but I can give you the blueprint—this book. In Part 1—Getting It—I'll talk you through learning to think like an entrepreneur. You'll learn what to expect and how to prepare yourself mentally for the work ahead. You'll pick up habits of thought and action that will compound your learning and make you more resilient to failure. You'll learn the habits and practices that help entrepreneurs succeed and to see themselves and their journeys in the most realistic and optimistic light. In Part 2—Doing It—you'll learn what branding is, why it matters, and how to create one of your own. I'll give you the basics of marketing and what's required for e-commerce. I'll offer recommendations about specific tools, explain my thinking, share the (often painful) experiences behind those recommendations, and I'll provide a basic how-to on their use. Finally, I'll give you a solid list of next steps and additional resources. It is as close as I can come to giving you everything you need to learn and do to start your own hair business.

If you're like me, I'll bet you want to skip straight to Part 2. Don't do it! I don't think there's another book out there that's as focused as this one on the specifics of how to start a hair business. I have tried to give you everything—all the steps and practical advice—you'll need, but none of it will do you any good if you're not thinking the right way about what you're doing. Nailing the big ideas of Part 1 can make the difference between success and failure, and it's the stuff no one ever talks about. If you didn't get it from the air around you growing up, you won't know it, and it will feel like an invisible canyon between you and your dreams. It's all the skills and ideas that I didn't know I needed to know, and if someone had sat me down and taught me at the beginning of my career, I'd already be retired and sitting on a yacht.

I've done what I set out to do. I built a business that was big enough and successful enough that I was able to take my mom's lifelong underlying fear of being broke and homeless away. In the next chapter, we'll talk about finding your why. She was mine, and I'm prouder of her fear-free years than of anything else I've done.

Mom died in January. It changed a lot of things for me. It shifted my focus from building a business to helping other people be successful in starting their own. I now run a wholesale operation that gives people one place to buy all the supplies they need, and our private Facebook group, https://hairbiz.tips/group, provides support and answers for a community of over 35,000 new entrepreneurs. I'm on there a lot, and at least once a week, someone sends me a DM packed with exclamation points saying they've just made their first sale. They're creating companies that change their lives selling products that help make people feel beautiful. Those messages are my new why.

Fearless Beauty is part of that why. So, if you're ready to start moving from where you are to that first sale, come join our Facebook group. It's private—just mention you're reading this book. And keep reading. There are ways of thinking about things and habits of mind that it took me years and a few lumps to learn. Successful businesspeople don't just do things differently; they think differently. You'll be way ahead of the game (and of where I was) if you can master these thinking tools now.

To become an entrepreneur and build your own hair business, you need to be fearless, and you need a blueprint. The next eight chapters are a blueprint. Getting fearless starts with believing it's possible. I'm making a great living in hair extensions as a forty-something, six-foot-three bald white man. Anything is possible.

Are you ready? Then let's get prepared.

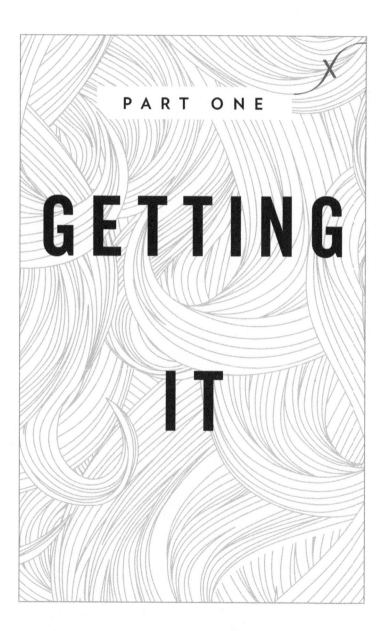

PART ONE

GETTING

IT

CHAPTER 1

GET PREPARED

In February of 2020, my girlfriend and I had spent the day in Vegas looking at spaces to open my second company's third location. We'd found a gorgeous one, and that night, we stood together on one of Aria's top floors, windows open, looking out on the lights. I opened my arms to the excitement and energy of the city like I could hold it all. "We could do really well here," I told Mary Margaret. She asked me what I wanted to do. I had no questions about that. I wanted to sign the lease. I wanted to jump straight into a future I saw shining as brightly as the skyline. It wasn't what I did.

Fourteen years earlier, in 2006, I'd started CurrySimple, my first business. I gave it everything I had, and it grew quickly. I got written up in magazines, and people I didn't know started coming up to me on the street to tell me how much they loved my curry. I was "the curry guy." Then 2008 hit and completely wiped me out.

One Friday, I booked my first flight to Thailand; the next Sunday, I had to call my grandmother and ask her to loan me enough to cover my butt. In 2009, I hadn't had enough experience with failure to feel anything but the rapid pulse of excitement on the threshold of something new and thrilling. I didn't notice the signs of the economic downturn looming large. I saw only promise in the future. In 2020, my vision was clearer.

Starting a business is exciting. You should be full of dreams and optimism about cool ideas you want to try out. Without that passion, you couldn't take that brave leap into something new. The start of anything is (and should be) thrilling, and running your own business is exciting. It can take you to the top of Las Vegas. But by the time I reached Aria, I'd been through enough darkness to see more than the lights. I could see the future—its promise *and* its dangers. The coronavirus had just started making the news that month, and I recognized signs I'd missed in 2008 of something big on the horizon. In 2020, I was excited, but I was also prepared.

You'll have to go get your own experience, but I can help you get prepared. I can't show you the future, but I can help you set realistic expectations and learn to read the signs that will show you what might be coming next.

If you're thinking seriously enough about starting your own business to be reading this book, I hope you're excited and passionate about working for yourself. Passion is the lighter fluid that gets the fire started. Preparation is the charcoal that cooks the meat. Be excited. Open your arms and hold them out to everything that's possible. Believe in the promise of your business. Then get prepared.

I wasn't prepared when I started CurrySimple. I wasn't clear on why I was starting a business—I just knew I wanted to. I didn't have clear goals, my expectations were wildly unrealistic, and I didn't have a plan. With Private Label Extensions, I had those things in place before I started, and the company did a lot better as a result. In this chapter, I'm going to talk you through everything that CurrySimple taught me I needed before I started another company. Your *why and* your goals will be unique to you, but I'll explain why you need to have them and how they can help. Having realistic expectations will keep you from getting discouraged and temper your goals. With a powerful *why* and goals that are ambitious but in line with reality, we'll take the final getting-prepared step—making a plan. Then, it will be your turn!

HAVE A WHY

Right now, you have a dream—and that's great. Maybe you can really see yourself running your own company, working for yourself, buying that new car. Maybe you've seen the Instagram stories of entrepreneurs who made it big and can imagine what it'd be like to have a life like theirs. Dreams are inspiring and full of energy and hope, and energy and hope can come in useful. But when you take that top-story view of the future, there's something even more important you need to look for. You need to see the *why* behind the dream.

Why do you want that dream you have to come true?

Even more than knowing what you want, knowing why will get you through the tough times. Sure, you want to be successful, you want to make big money. Why? What would that money do for you?

Want to work for yourself? Why? My bet is when you really think about it, your *why* isn't about you. It's about creating something special or changing something for somebody else. Why do you get up in the morning now? Yeah, you have to go to work to pay rent. Why? Is it to prove something to yourself or to someone else? To make a nice place for your kids? To never need to ask Grandma for a loan?

I've helped a lot of people start their own hair businesses, and I've seen many of them obtain the success they sought, and when they've been heart-to-heart honest with themselves, their *why* has always been about another person. Maybe you want to give your kids more financial stability. Maybe you want to give your sister a job. Maybe you want to help other women feel beautiful. It's not that you don't want nice things for yourself, but you want them for other people, too, right? Starting a business is hard. It requires time and money and sacrifice, and if you're only working for a yacht-sailing version of Future You, on the tough days, Current You is going to seem just as deserving of a day off, and you're going to let her off the hook. Some days, it's not going to feel worth it to keep going just for you. On those days, knowing who else you're doing it for is the only thing that keeps you going.

HAVE GREAT GOALS

If you don't know where you're going, you won't know when you get there. You've got to set goals so you know what success looks like. Big goals are inspiring and energizing, and energy can be hard to come by sometimes. I had the goal of making Mom feel safe. Maybe you have a goal that comes out of your *why*. Maybe you want to make a million dollars. (That was one of mine, too.)

Making a million dollars is a fine goal. Making a million dollars in four years is a better one because four years from now, you'll know if you hit your target or not. Goals are better when they have numbers—dollars, years, locations—anything you can count. Things other people could measure. This is why happiness (although great) isn't a great goal. Making a million dollars in four years is a goal that might not guarantee your happiness, but it probably wouldn't damage it much.

Making a million dollars in four years is a goal a lot of people have, but most of them don't make it in part because it isn't *actionable*. In a minute, we'll talk about how to gauge whether a goal is realistic, but first, you need to set a goal you can act on. Do this by asking yourself a series of, "What's the first step?" questions. *If I want to make a million dollars selling hair, what's the first step?* Selling hair, right? But that's a goal without numbers, so you need to drill deeper. *If I want to sell hair, what's my first step?* Making your first sale. "Make my first sale," is a good start. (And making your first sale may actually feel better than making your first million, so it still works if you're aiming for "happy" instead of "rich.") Now your goal is actionable. Make it measurable. "Make my first sale four months from today." Now that's a great goal!

Making your first sale is a huge accomplishment. Most people will never start a business, never have a website, never get a single person to go to their website, put something in their shopping cart, and click "buy." For most people, that first sale (like that million) is just a dream, but for you, it's a goal. It's actionable and measurable. But is it realistic?

HAVE REALISTIC EXPECTATIONS

The difference between a dream and a vision is whether your eyes are open or shut. A dream is something you make up out of your imagination. A vision is something you see clearly. In dreams, you go from one location to another without traveling—you're just suddenly there. A vision sees the goal and the steps between.

"And they lived happily ever after" is a dream. Recommitting every day is a vision.

EXPECT IT TO TAKE TWO YEARS

Overnight success is a dream. Instagram is full of stories about businesses that blew up overnight, but if that's your plan, you might as well play the lottery. The odds are about the same. Realistically, while everyone's timeline is different, you should expect it to take about two years of hard and consistent effort before you can start taking money out of the business to pay yourself or take a vacation. If you make it sooner than that, good for you! But expect and plan for success to take two years.

Expect for it to take many of the hours and most of your brain in those two years, and tell the people in your life to expect the same. Expect them to struggle with this. Talk to your friends and family now and let them know you're not going to be as available to them. If you have a serious romantic partner, talk to them a couple of times. They'll want to support you, and they'll say that they do, but it can be hard for them to imagine what that means on the day-to-day, need-to-miss-dinner, can't-go-on-vacation level.

PARTNER TO PARTNER

My long-time girlfriend has written a letter of sympathy and advice to anyone in your life who's likely to be impacted by your new entrepreneurial venture. You can read it at the end of this chapter and download it from our website to send to the people who love (and will soon miss) you. https://hairbiz.tips/partner.

EXPECT TO WALK BEFORE YOU RUN

My goal for this year (2020) was to do eight figures. (It's November, and I've already reached it!) Why wasn't it nine? Because I haven't learned how to be a nine-figure entrepreneur yet. I'm not ready. It'd be too big a jump. I know I have to go through all the stages to get there. Nine figures, and I'd probably implode. Expect to get one sale a week before you get one every day. Expect to level up, and expect it to take time each time you do. You have to learn how to be an entrepreneur. Then you have to learn how to break even. Then you have to learn how to turn a profit. I understand the desire to skip steps, to go right from where you are to where you want to be. It's an appealing dream. Recognize it for what it is. Then wake up, and get to work.

EXPECT IT TO BE EMOTIONAL

Entrepreneurship is not for everyone. I know plenty of people who tried it and are now much happier working a regular job without all the emotional highs and lows that come with starting your own company and working for yourself. There's no disgrace in taking the entrepreneur road and deciding to change direction along the way. The world needs both entrepreneurs and non-entrepreneurs, and neither brings shame or glory as long as you're doing what you're best suited to. I'm an entrepreneur, but the qualities that make me one aren't what I look for when I hire.

The old cliché is that entrepreneurship is an emotional rollercoaster. It is. The trick is to remember that a rollercoaster *is a ride*. You chose to get on it knowing it was going to drag you up slowly and throw you down fast. Expect it. It's a little less scary if you've got your eyes open and can see what's ahead.

You will get emotional about it because you care. Having big feelings is human. It's part of what keeps you motivated, but you've got to manage them. I'll always remember getting that first order from a non-family member. I did all the packing and shipping for CurrySimple on an old table under the intermittent glow of fluorescent lights in my chilly basement, but while I packed that non-family order, I was dancing around like it was a disco. Not much in life feels better than a win you worked hard for and gave up things to get. The next week I got my first charge-back because the shipping company lost the package, and I was just as freaked out in the opposite direction.

I don't freak out anymore. The wins and losses are even bigger, but it's been a long time since I danced in the cellar. I've gotten used to the ride. I've been around the track enough times to know what's coming. It's why I didn't take that gorgeous retail space in Vegas. I'm not an emotionless robot. Far from it. It's more like I'm the guy designing the rollercoaster, not the one riding it. I get excited planning the big rise and drop. I enjoy it, but I don't feel every bump and jolt all the way up my spine anymore. And that's a good thing. Backs don't get younger with time.

Rules of the Ride

There are a couple of things I've trained myself to do to handle the highs and lows of entrepreneurship because they never stop coming.

Wait

Unless there's fire or blood, you don't need to react right away. This is especially true when dealing with customers. You will get a bad review one day. People will write you nasty emails complaining and blaming you for things—some of which are completely out of your control. You will want to shoot them a quick reply. Don't do it. Unless it's a quick, "Oh, wow, thanks so much, your review/comment/email totally made my day" reply, don't respond immediately. If you're angry or upset, even if it's completely justifiable, put some time between your private, personal reaction, and your public, professional one. Companies don't have feelings. You do, but when you're being the voice of your company, you need to keep your emotions out of it. Make a rule for yourself to wait before you react to anything negative. Time is usually enough to mellow the feelings, and then you can decide on the best action instead of letting the negative reaction decide for you.

Q&A

What if there's a negative review sitting out there on the web for everyone to see? Don't I need to respond quickly?

No.

Yes, an unanswered review might look bad, but an emotional reply looks much worse. A bad review doesn't make you look bad. A bad response will.

Reframe

Find another way to think about whatever has upset you. When you get a negative review, remember—you can't please everyone. If you're not getting the occasional bad review, you're not selling enough hair. Try looking at negative comments as a positive sign that you're reaching a wider range of customers. And pay attention when a customer might have a good point and there's something you need to change within your business. Negative reviews (while never much fun) can be a great source of customer feedback that will end up helping you keep growing your business!

When you make an expensive or embarrassing mistake, try to tell yourself you've just learned something to avoid in the future. The pain you're feeling will help you remember.

Every problem is a chance to take your problem-solving skills to a higher level. Every bad day is practice at pushing through bad days. Every screw-up is a lesson.

Remember Your Why

Whether it's a bad review or numbers that missed your target or some random, unlucky thing that hit you for no reason, take a minute to reconnect with your why. You didn't start your own company because you wanted to never hear anything negative or to always be right or never get a bad break. You started your business to do something bigger for yourself and for other people. It's worth dealing with the little bad things to get the bigger good ones.

EXPECT TO SACRIFICE

I work an eighty-hour week. (It's not all physical work at this point, but much of it is mental and strategizing for future business moves.) For me, the sacrifices I'm making in the quality of my life right now are worth it, but it's important for everyone, before they start this journey, to check in with themselves. Honestly evaluate how the long days and emotional upheavals you're signing up for align with everything else you want to do in your life. Have this day of reckoning with yourself now because it's unavoidable. If you don't do it now, you'll end up doing it later with more on the line and years and dollars already invested. Are you able to make the investment of time and money necessary to get your hair business off the ground and active? Are you ready to risk those investments on something that might not work out? My first business failed. Many first businesses do. Even first-time entrepreneurs who are successful experience losses in the first couple of years. If you're not okay with all that right now, this might not be the right time for you to start your own business.

EXPECT PROBLEMS

Something is going to go wrong. Several somethings. This makes you like everyone else who's ever been successful in business. You're in great company! If nothing ever goes wrong, you're probably not pushing yourself hard enough. (Or you're a freak. You don't want to be a freak, do you?) When you realize you've made a mistake or when something goes wrong for no reason at all, remember: at least you're not a freak. Nobody is 100 percent 100 percent of the time.

- You will have bad days.
- You will get bad reviews.
- Your shipping carrier will lose your package.
- You will miss some of your goals.
- You will get discouraged, overwhelmed, angry, scared, and/or frustrated.

These problems are only problems if you let them stop you. If you don't, they're just great practice.

EXPECT TO PRACTICE

Starting your own company is a lot like starting anything else. You're not going to be good at it right away. You don't expect to pick up a guitar for the first time and play like Jimi Hendrix. It takes practice to excel at entrepreneurship. Everything you do will take longer than you expect the first couple of times, but you'll get faster. You'll avoid lots of beginner mistakes having read this book because I've already made them for you. But you're a creative person; you'll find some of your very own to make. Be patient with yourself. Remember, you're doing this for the first time. You're learning, and learning is work.

EXPECT YOUR FRIENDS TO BE FRIENDS

Friends are friends; they aren't customers. Don't start a business expecting your friends and family will be your customer base. Don't even expect them to be your first sale. Your friends probably won't buy from you. I don't know why, but I've seen it happen so many times that I can tell you it isn't personal. Richard McDonald's friends probably didn't eat his burgers either. It doesn't mean anything about your future success or the quality of your products. Don't let it hurt your feelings. It isn't about you. It's just the way it is.

EXPECT SLOW PERIODS

When I started Private Label Extensions, I already knew a lot about launching and running a small business, and I avoided many of the mistakes I made with CurrySimple. Our first month was great. Our second month was better. Then we had three slow months in a row. It was scary. Later, I learned that our sales always fall off during the summer. I hadn't known to expect that, but because I was prepared for slow periods, we got through our first summer just fine. I've since learned to prepare for the summer months by hoarding cash in the spring like some kind of reverse squirrel.

In 2016, after I'd *finally* started taking a salary, we hit another slow period, and I went a month without paying myself because I had employees to pay and was out of operating cash.

When businesses get into trouble, they typically start making cuts to their biggest expenses, and for me, that would mean staff. I've been an employee, and I know what it's like to feel your job isn't secure so I'm extremely careful to avoid the kind of risks that would mean I had to cut staff positions during the slower months. (Being responsible for the livelihood of staff is a big responsibility and one I take very seriously.)

EXPECT TO PUT THE COMPANY FIRST

It sounds a little backward, but the best way to take care of yourself is to put your company ahead of yourself. I worked for more than two and a half years and hired three people before I paid myself anything for my work at Private Label Extensions. I was employee number four because I wanted to give the company a solid foundation. For the first two years, I got up at five every morning to work on the company before I went to my day job. I'd work all day, come home and work until midnight. If I'd been thinking about what was best for me, I wouldn't have done that. By thinking about what was best for Private Label Extensions, I built a company that takes pretty good care of me (and about thirty other people).

Expect to spend both time and money on your company before you spend much of either on yourself. With the money I have in the bank right now, I could go out tomorrow and buy a Lamborghini for cash. I'm buying the company more real estate instead. It's less fun, but I look at it as treating myself—not to an excellent car but to a decent night's sleep. I've had enough experience with failure to feel pretty decadent protecting myself against ever having to borrow money from a family member again.

In a perfect world, you won't augment your personal income with your business's income until you can afford to pay yourself every month, at least as much as you're making right now. Of course, the world isn't perfect, and you won't be able to keep reinvesting everything your business makes and spending none of it on yourself for the full two to three years it'll take to get it established. My advice: buy yourself new tires if you need them but not a new car (and maybe never the Lamborghini).

The only exception to this—and it isn't really an exception—is money you don't spend on more inventory or anything else your business needs, but which you save as a safety net for your company. I'd recommend having enough saved to cover all your business expenses for at least three, but ideally for six months, as an insurance policy against slow periods, mistakes, and unlucky breaks. Think about it as buying sleep. The better buffer you have against things going wrong—and you should expect them to—the less you'll stress each time life meets that expectation or fails to meet your more optimistic ones.

Being one mistake away from broke isn't good for your peace of mind. The safety net is good for your business *because* it's good for your stress levels and lets you try the double-flip instead of sticking with the single. It turns the question, "What would you do if you knew you could not fail?" into, "What would you do if you knew failure was survivable?" I bet the answer to both is something really cool, but only the second is possible. Failure is always an option.

We'll talk more about surviving failure in the next chapter, but believe me, avoiding is better than surviving, and putting the company first works like garlic on the failure vampire. I think of it like this: how much pain can you stand for how long? How long can you stand to pay yourself nothing? How long can you deny yourself a vacation? Celebrate the stuffing out of every success, but delay rewarding yourself with money or time for as long as you can.

> More pain now means less pain later.

The inability to put your company first is so common that long-time business leaders and the people who study them have a term for the entrepreneurs who can't do it—selfish owners. Selfish owners feed off their companies instead of nurturing them. They start taking too much out too soon. They make decisions based on what makes them happy or looks great on their Instagram. They think the rules don't apply to them and that they shouldn't have to suffer like the rest of us. Don't be that guy.

EXPECT PAIN

The pain of entrepreneurship comes in several flavors. There's the stomach- and shoulder-knotting anxiety over how it's doing and whether you're good enough to pull off what you're trying to do. There's the gnawing grumble of impatience that none of it is happening fast enough. There's the empty feeling of hours not spent doing something fun or relaxing, and the simple pale exhaustion of having spent them all on hard work instead. But maybe the most dangerous pain of entrepreneurship is the prickling envies. They break out in rashes of defiance and doubt. And they're symptoms of Instagram abuse.

Instagram is a marketing tool. It's not a success gauge. If you try to measure how well you're doing by looking at the social media of other entrepreneurs, you'll catch the envies like a fever. The envies will tell you you've worked hard, and you're starting to make good money. You deserve some of the nice things you see other successful entrepreneurs enjoying. You'll start to believe that you're seeing the whole story—that starting a business has been easier or faster or more glamorous for all these other people than it has for you.

The envies will distract you with accomplishments that are outside of your goals and convince you to start working against yourself by chasing dreams that have nothing to do with your *why* and everything to do with someone else's fantasy. Expect the pain, and learn to answer envy with the pride you take in being able to put up with more and wait longer than anyone else. Let them be the ones who get distracted by all the outside signs of success. Let them get addicted to having people tell them how great they're doing. It'll never heal their envies. And you will have already gotten over yours and moved on.

EXPECT TO SAY NO (A LOT)

"No" is one of the powerful words in business. Saying "no" is usually part of putting your company first. You have to say "no" to:

- Friends who want you to come out with them Saturday night instead of staying home working on your business.
- The new pair of shoes or the big birthday party instead of spending the money on additional advertising.
- That third cocktail or the heavy meal that's going to make you sluggish the next day.
- The guy who burns up your brain cycles.
- The friend who always brings the drama.
- The Netflix binge.
- The snooze bar.
- Giving back.

This is a special kind of saying "no" that most people don't anticipate and that even the most hard-working struggle with. When you start to have some success, people will start asking you for help or advice. Saying no can feel really selfish, but it isn't. Not giving anything away now will put you in the position to make a much bigger difference later. Bill Gates gave away $589 million last year. That's enough to pay someone $157 a minute (or $9,420 an hour) every minute for the next fifty years—even while they're asleep. But even Bill recommends being really selfish during the early years of your business. I'm not saying to wait until you've made your first billion to start giving back, but you are going to have to get used to saying "no" to requests for help.

Hey! I know you are busy but can you show me how to grow my business?

No. Sorry!

I love helping people, but I've gotten really good at turning down requests from people asking for my help. I didn't give a cent or a second away the first couple of years, but now Private Label Extensions and I personally both give back to the community. We donate wigs to cancer patients and laptops to Black entrepreneur organizations. But one of my favorite ways to give back is to post to Facebook and offer to take a young entrepreneur to lunch. I've got to stop working to eat anyway, and if I can also use that time to give someone a leg up, I'm happy to do it.

EXPECT DIFFERENT EXPECTATIONS

Have I scared you? Has all the time and patience and big feelings, and sacrifice and problems and pain and practice and slow periods I've told you to expect left you thinking entrepreneurship sounds like more trouble than it's worth? Don't quit on me yet! Hardcore entrepreneurship isn't the only kind out there. There are different ways of dancing with entrepreneurship, and the expectations are different for each.

The Side Hustle

If you love your job, if you like the stability of having a regular paycheck you know you can count on, or if you're at a place where you can't afford a serious investment of time and money, you can still be an entrepreneur. With a side hustle, you're working to reach a certain level of success or a set amount of additional income and then to hold it steady there. You don't want to keep growing your business and take it as far as it can go. This is a completely legitimate form of entrepreneurship. Starting your own company is definitely not for everyone! Having a side hustle is more comfortable, but you get out what you put in. A side hustle takes less out of you, but you'll make less in the long run.

Everything we've talked about so far, and all the material in the rest of the book still apply, but if you want a side hustle, not a business, your mindset will be a little different. Side hustle thinking sounds like this: I don't want to dedicate my life to starting a company right now, and I don't want all the stress, but if I could make an extra $500 to $1,000 a month, that'd be pretty cool.

With a side hustle, you still work hard, but you reinvest less. You still make sacrifices but for a shorter period of time, and you put that initial investment of time and money in expecting to get it back sooner.

The Full Tango

If your goal is to quit your job and run a company where you work full-time and to grow that company as big as it can get, you'll need to put more on the line. Full Tango thinking sounds like this: "I'm ready to dedicate everything to starting my own business. I'm going to give it everything I've got and keep giving." When you go this route, you don't pay yourself anything until you can afford to quit your job and go full-time at your business. Until then, you work two full-time jobs, and when you quit, you work the same eighty-plus hours at your business and take on the risk of having your business support you and solve your own health insurance, retirement savings, and taxes. You pay yourself modestly, don't give yourself raises, and keep reinvesting everything in your business.

The Half-*ss Shuffle

If you want to fall on your face, this is the path for you. Quit your job right now to work full-time on starting your business. Please don't do this. I think it's probably the single biggest business mistake you can make for several reasons.

Working full-time for yourself requires setting your own deadlines, scheduling your time, and being much more efficient with both time and money than anyone knows how to do if they're used to working for someone else. You have to be better than the best boss you ever had and a better employee than you've ever been. And you have to hit the road running at that speed. Even after having started CurrySimple and run it successfully for several years, I didn't go this route when I started Private Label Extensions. I worked a full-time job, *and* I worked full-time on my business.

Going full-time at a company that doesn't exist yet pushes the stress dial into the red zone. You simply cannot make good business decisions when the stakes are that high. Don't put yourself in the position of feeding yourself or your business.

The Change-Up

You can rev up a side hustle into a full-time gig or downshift the opposite direction. I've seen both scenarios work out well. Sometimes, especially when their kids are small, people will work a full-time job and have a side hustle that brings in a nice supplemental income. Later, maybe with their kids in school, they'll shift gears, stop taking the money out of the business, and start working full-time at both jobs with the goal of getting and keeping it growing.

I've also seen people dance as hard as they can for a couple of years trying to be a full-time entrepreneur and decide to go the side hustle route. Sometimes, they do this before the company gets to the place where they can quit their other job, and sometimes, they work full-time at their own company for a few years and go back to working full- or part-time for someone else. It's all good. Except the shuffle. Don't do that.

HAVE A PLAN

Once you have a why, goals, and realistic expectations, you need a plan—a realistic plan to achieve your goals and serve your *why*.

The difference between a goal and a plan is the difference between A→Z and A→B→C all the way to Z. There are a couple of reasons to have both. A goal keeps you focused; a plan tells you what to focus on next.

Plans keep you from getting distracted. If Z is your goal and 8 comes along (and eight is all sexy with its curves and loops), you might want to do eight. Eight might even feel like it could get you to Z. Only if you have a plan that says after A you do B, and after B you do C, can you look at 8, and realize it's a distraction. It might be fun, but it's not part of your plan. Maybe later, you'll decide you want to go 1→10, and then 8 will have its moment, but for now, if getting your first sale is your goal, and having your own website up and running in ninety days is Z, anything that doesn't move you along the alphabet is off your list and needs to wait.

This is why it's important to write down every step, every letter. Whether you're going to execute on each one yourself or, once you have staff, have someone else knocking down some tasks for you, get everything you need to do written down, and then do the next thing, no matter what.

> Write down everything!

If your goal is to launch your own hairline, plan *not* to start a make-up line, a clothing brand, and a shoe company for the next couple of years. Planning what you're not going to do and planning not to do what doesn't move you toward your goal makes it easier to say no to things that might otherwise divert time or money away from your goal.

- Plan to spend $1,000 a month for two years.*
- Plan to spend at least two hours a day six days a week
- Plan to spend your lunch break, your commute, and your time in the shower thinking about your business.
- Plan to sequence your goals. I recommend this order: Launch your website. Get your first sale. Get your first $1,000 in sales. Have your first profitable month.**
- Plan to move fast.

*If you don't have $1,000 a month you can set aside to spend on your business every month, you can still get one started, but plan on spending more time—closer to four hours a day every day—and to take three or four years to turn a profit instead of two or three.

**Yes, you'll learn about each of these steps in the book.

HABITS

Habits are plans you set up like automatic bill pay. They let you pre-make good decisions. Start building new habits today. You've already read the first chapter of this book. Make a habit of reading at least a little more every day or spending the same amount of time doing the Your Turn exercises at the end of each chapter. Daily habits leverage the superpower of consistency and make it stronger. (We'll talk more about the importance of consistency in chapter 2.) Make a plan right now to start a habit of spending at least two hours a day, six days a week on your business. For the next three chapters, plan to spend that time with this book. When you hit Part 2, you'll start spending more time doing things like picking your company name and building your website. I'll take you through all of it, step-by-step, but the first step is starting the habit of taking those steps.

Start building the habit of using a calendar and a budget.

Start building the habit of working on your business every day.

> **PRO TIP**
>
> Money isn't everything, but it's your company's blood. You can lose some for a while, but if too much goes too fast, you're in trouble. Once you start spending money, you need to start a timer in your head to measure how long you have before you bleed out or need a transfusion.

START NOW AND DON'T STOP

Starting a business is like starting a mower. Getting going can be really tough, but by the time you've gotten it started and mowed the first couple of feet, as long as you keep pushing it along, it'll keep going. If you stop—even just to go inside for a drink of water—you've got to do all the string-yanking to get it going again. Do everything you can to keep from stalling. Guard your momentum with your life! And if you run out of gas, get back to it as soon as you can. Only stopping and staying stopped is fatal.

START HERE

Starting a business is hard, but we've created a system that smooths out a lot of the lumps and helps you avoid the biggest mistakes. There's no easier way to get into the hair business. So get started. Here. Now.

YOUR TURN: GET PREPARED

Get a notebook. I recommend having one that's just for your business and keeping it with you all the time. Use it to help you get into the habit of writing everything down and of working on or thinking about your business all (or at least a lot) of the time.

IDENTIFY YOUR WHY

Think about your big why. What is going to make all the work worthwhile? When you feel like quitting, what will inspire you to keep going?

My first why was my mom. Now I have two: a client-based why and a staff-based one. I'm very motivated by my desire to make a difference in people's lives by helping them be successful in the beauty industry. It's also really important to me to be the boss I always wanted to have.

A good why is more about creating change for other people than it is about getting stuff for yourself.

Put your why on the first page of your notebook. Write a few sentences if you want to, but try distilling it down into one that feels powerful. Pictures are even better. If you're doing this for your kids, put their picture on the first page of your notebook. If you're doing it to afford your own house, find a picture of a house to put there. If you're starting a hair business because you want to have created something amazing that helps women feel beautiful, find a picture that represents that.

(Want to share your why? Leave a comment here: https://hairbiz.tips/why)

WRITE DOWN YOUR GOALS

I recommend setting sales goals. Without sales, there's no company. If it's easier to think up other business goals like getting your first part-time employee or moving more of what you sell from drop-shipping to inventory (more about this in chapter 4), it's easy to turn those goals into sales goals by asking yourself what you'd need to be making in sales to accomplish them.

Goals that are about things like getting your website launched or creating your first ads are also sales goals because they're the things you need to do to get sales.

In your notebook, write down goals that inspire you. I think getting your first sale is a great one. Add numbers to your goals. How many, how long, by when? Remember, good goals are objective. They're targets anyone could look at and know whether or not you've hit them.

SET REALISTIC EXPECTATIONS

Look at the goal with the nearest "by when" date and test it with the reality checks I gave you. If you're going with the goal of having your first sale in ninety days, ask yourself if you're ready to put in the time, make the sacrifices, and spend the money. It's hard to really commit to a goal if you don't believe it's possible. Testing your goals to make sure they're realistic and changing those that aren't achievable—not easily but still do-ably—is critical.

Look at your calendar. When are you going to work on your

business? Find at least two hours a day, six days a week that you can schedule right now, and block those times on your calendar.

Look at your budget. What are you spending money on now that you can earmark for this instead? Do you have some savings you can spend? Can you cut out some things or cut back on others? Tag that money for your business now.

What will your business budget be? How much can you afford as an initial investment? How much are you going to spend on it every month? Write it down. "My company's initial investment is $____ and our monthly budget is $____" and make sure you know where that money is coming from.

Once you know why you're doing this and that and you have the time and money to make it happen, commit. Write it in your notebook.

MAKE A PLAN

Once you have time and money allocated, you need to know what to do with them. I'll take you through every step you'll need to take, so you don't have to have the whole plan in your notebook yet, but do make a plan to use the time you've blocked off to work on your business to start moving through the chapters and doing the steps they lay out.

Get a planner. Write in your plan for finishing this book. If you start saving money and putting in your two hours a day beginning tomorrow, you can realistically plan to finish the next two chapters in a week.

NOW YOU'RE PREPARED!

Being prepared means having more than a dream. You need some idea of what to expect—both good and bad and have time and money earmarked for working on your business. You need to have put the right habits in place, know what you're working toward and why it matters. Be fearless!

Once you know what to expect, you're not done learning. In fact, once you get the next chapter right, you're never done.

PARTNER TO PARTNER

Dear To-Be-Entrepreneur's Partner,

Being in any relationship is tough if you actually put in the work, no matter how short or long you've been with someone. Having an entrepreneur as a partner is an even harder one that I was definitely not prepared to welcome into my life. I had no idea what I was in for before I met Michael, who was an even crazier version of a regular entrepreneur. He's a serial entrepreneur. Yikes! I feel like taking this journey with him is like a very rocky roller coaster ride that often breaks down while you're upside down on the tracks.

I've never been exposed to the entrepreneurial life before Michael. I was a full-time student working in retail when I first met him. I've worked retail and food service jobs since I was fourteen years old. I've always craved stability and security ever since my family and I came here from the Philippines. My mom was a single parent who only had $150 in her pocket with four kids in tow who were all ages ten and under when we landed here. We came to America to start a new life, but of course that also meant starting from scratch. My mom didn't even know how to drive at the age of thirty-nine! Talk about truly starting from scratch! She was and still is one of the hardest working people I've ever met. I witnessed her sacrifice everything to keep us happy, safe, and healthy while juggling two to three jobs. Coming from that, I knew I wanted to pursue a career that gave me purpose but also a solid foundation, so I could have a stable and secure life that allowed me to be there for my family when they needed me. I went to school to pursue my passion in dietetics, become a registered dietitian, and work in a hospital, which is what I'm doing now.

Man, did I pick a partner who was the complete opposite of the life I wanted in many ways! I love the nine-to-five life! It's the kind of career path that seems like the nemesis of entrepreneurs from what I've noticed over the years. The nine-to-five is often looked down upon by the entrepreneurial community, but I truly believe that everyone thrives in different environments. I like being able to separate my work and life. That balance is very important to me. Being able to leave my work at the hospital as soon as I clock out is a great fit for my mental health. My career is stable and secure.

I don't have to worry about gambling with high-risk, high-reward decisions. I just need a career I love and enough money to cover my basic needs, so I can focus on experiences with my partner, friends, and family that truly make me happy. Growing up as a low-income immigrant in America makes you realize the importance of meeting our basic needs: access to affordable housing, nutritious food, healthcare, education, and not living paycheck to paycheck.

There wasn't a lot I needed or wanted in my life. Security and stability were two of my biggest goals, so meeting Michael, who was basically the antithesis of those things in many ways, was really terrifying. He had crazy and humongous ideas that scared me. He would risk so much time, money, and effort—pretty much everything—to execute them. There was no line between work and life. His work seeped into every aspect of our life—meals, get-togethers, vacations, etc. It was never-ending. He worked all hours of days and nights. Every business he started was a gamble. I never knew if they would ever take off. Everything was always riding a fine line between success and failure. He lost everything when CurrySimple failed when I met him, and he was willing to risk it all again for another business venture. It was mind-boggling. Meanwhile, I'm just in a corner, rocking back and forth hoping we'd have enough money to pay our bills and put food on the table while I was still in school. I was so grateful when I started my career in the hospital. At that point, at least one of us had a stable career to cover both of our basic needs just in case his businesses didn't take. That gave me some peace of mind.

Even now that he's insanely successful, I have the same fears and face the same obstacles. I don't think that those ever really go away when your partner is an entrepreneur. After being together for ten years, I've learned to be a better partner to someone who is an entrepreneur, and Michael learned to be a better partner to someone who isn't. Here are some ways we've been able to navigate through the tough obstacles we have and still face together that may help someone who is dating an entrepreneur for the first time. Of course, everyone and every partnership is different, but these are what helped me and our relationship learn, grow, and become stronger for the past decade.

- There were a lot of times when priority for the business preceded everything else, and our relationship was no exception to that. I have to constantly remind Michael that our relationship is a priority. It can be easy for him to get lost in just hunkering down and putting all of his time and effort into the business. I understand the difficult choices and sacrifices that he has to make on a daily basis, but our relationship is just as important. Simply put in my mind, every relationship we choose to have in our lives is just like having a plant. In order to thrive, it has to be consistently nurtured. You can't just disappear and hope it survives without proper care and attention.

- I set boundaries in the very beginning also as our relationship went through changes and growth, and I held Michael accountable. Being so vocal about my expectations and what I needed out of the relationship was intimidating at first, but he's not a mind reader. It was only fair to communicate those things in order to set him and our relationship up for success. Playing guessing games wasn't going to cut it especially with his already daunting responsibilities as an entrepreneur.

- Making time for our relationship—big and small—is crucial and goes back to making it a priority. Entrepreneurs have the tendency to sacrifice a lot, which can include our relationship. It's often a big-risk, big-reward mindset and our relationship was definitely in that line of fire. Skipping a date night or an activity we're supposed to do together here and there can be detrimental. Once you start letting things slide, it can turn into a habit. Our relationship wasn't built on grand spectacular events. Yes, we had a lot of big hurdles we overcame, but it was also the small things that really solidified our relationship. Even if we do have to push off time spent together, we always make sure to reschedule follow-through.

- Compromise, compromise, compromise. I think we all have our list of deal breakers in relationships, but beyond that, it's all about meeting someone halfway. Again, Michael and I are complete opposites in every way imaginable—from little things like temperature, weather, food, music, movies, fashion, etc., all the way to bigger things like communication, ways of giving and receiving love, problem-solving, etc. But we've learned to always make concessions and find a good medium to keep each other happy. It's rare that we ever choose to be stubborn. That doesn't really get us anywhere. He likes comic books, so I go to comic book stores with him. I like scary movies, so he watches them even with a lot of regret.

- Active listening has been a saving grace for our relationship. It took a while to put into practice. In the beginning, I felt like we were just talking at each other whether it was about something simple like what we wanted to eat all the way to bigger arguments, and we were just each waiting for the other person to finish so we could have our say. It's always something we're working on. Growing up, my mom was constantly repeating herself to my dad, and eventually I realized that she kept doing that, because she felt like no one was listening. It was a hard realization, and I didn't want me or Michael to ever feel that way. If ever it does happen, I point it out. I don't want to be in a relationship with two broken records stuck on repeat.

- Communication. Why are we so bad at it? This has been really tough. Michael and I communicate in VERY different ways. As extroverted as he is, he's often the quiet one in arguments. I have social anxiety, but I'm very confrontational and have word vomit. I like to talk it out and find a solution as soon as possible. Michael likes to sleep on it and then forget it ever happened. We're just so different, but all it takes is dedication and work. It all comes back to compromise and active listening. I also think what's often forgotten is learning how your partner receives information. We've both had to learn and adapt to communicating things in a way that the other person actually understands and absorbs. That's been extremely helpful.

- I made sure that we are both very independent in many ways and have a life outside of each other. He has his set of friends and I have mine. I have my career and he has his businesses. We have different hobbies and interests. We have the same overarching goals and values, but other than that we pretty much do our own thing besides the allotted time we set aside for our relationship. They say long-term partners tend to look alike after a while since we start to adopt each other's mannerisms and quirks, but Michael and I could not be any further from that since we have our own lives. That has definitely attributed to the longevity of our relationship and has kept our relationship interesting over the past decade.

- I learned to be comfortable with not being Michael's hype man as his partner. His ideas can be so wild, so I do my best to help tame and polish them. It's hard for him to take criticism at times, but I noticed that at the top of his game, there's not a lot of people willing to tell him the truth and make him face reality. I have to hold him accountable. One of my roles as his partner is to be completely honest with him even if he might not like what I'm saying. I may be one of his biggest fans, but that doesn't mean that I'm his hype person. I often challenge him in how he can better execute his ideas that would be best not just for him but also his team and his clients, and sometimes that means being brutally honest.

This journey has been incredibly tough. We reach our breaking point at least once a year from the incredible pressures of the entrepreneurial life on top of the normal ones from being in a relationship in general. I honestly didn't know what I was signing up for. It was hard for Michael to share it with someone who comes from a different mindset, but we are truly partners in every way. We dedicate time and effort to each other just as we do in our careers. I never thought I'd live the amazing life I'm living now. Just like the high risk Michael takes every day, I took one, too, by choosing this life with him.

The high reward when it does finally pay off is unimaginable. I honestly never really believed it until it came. I don't have the same mind as Michael. He's the most positive person I've ever met. He says he's his own number one fan. I'm a realist, who borderlines pessimism. I just supported him and did everything I could to help him in his journey. I've been to places, met people, and done things I would never have been able to do if I played it safe. I'm grateful for the privileges it's afforded us so we can live a good life and also use it to help our family, friends, and the community along the way. We took a chance on each other regardless of our endless differences. All of the extraordinary things we've experienced has been worth every ounce of pain we've endured. I am truly humbled and forever grateful to Michael. He's truly a good and kind man who sees the best in people and all situations. We complete each other, and I'm proud to have him as my partner in life.

Good luck!

Mary Margaret

CHAPTER 2

GET THINKING

I remember walking down the aisle of a crowded plane past the people in the spacious first-class seats, who were already reading their books or working on their laptops while the rest of us were trying to find space for our bags. With my six-foot-three self uncomfortably folded into a last row seat whose back didn't even recline, I had plenty of questions: *Why are those people in first class and I'm all the way back here? What's so special about them? Who do they think they are?*

Then I asked the entrepreneurial question: *How?*

How did they get there? *How* is the question that turns envy into education. The answer to the how question gives you instructions, and it's the way entrepreneurs look at everything.

You can become an entrepreneur without thinking like one—I know I did—but it wasn't until I started thinking like one that I became successful. No, this isn't more "think and grow rich" BS, where I tell you to sit on the sofa and imagine great stacks of cash. It's almost the opposite. To think like an entrepreneur, you don't visualize anything. You start asking the right questions and building the right thinking habits.

GET CURIOUS

Curiosity is the defining feature of entrepreneurial thinking. I know I've always asked lots of questions about things; you probably have, too, at least when you were a child. But if you're like I was, the questions you ask aren't always the big entrepreneurial one. It took me a long time to figure it out, and it wasn't a sudden lightning strike of insight.

OBSERVATION AND ANALYSIS

The first step of curiosity is simply noticing things in the world around you. A lot of people walk through life, looking only down at their feet and into their own heads. Entrepreneurs look at things the way detectives do.

> Entrepreneurs investigate life.

I'm not saying this is a natural (or even normal) way of being. You have to train yourself to notice more and different things. Notice which of the businesses that you see every day are doing well and which are struggling. Notice how your experience varies in different restaurants or stores. Notice which marketing emails you read and which you ignore. Every time you think, *That was cool!* or, *That sucked!* notice your reactions. If you don't recognize when something different or interesting is going on, you're missing out on the chance to learn something from everything. Train yourself to make these kinds of observations and write them down.

Then start asking *how?*

Your first *how* is almost always going to be: *How did they do that?* That's a fantastic place to begin your entrepreneurial detective work. Figure out the big pieces and then ask the entrepreneurial *how?* Again, break the answers down into smaller, less abstract, more comprehendible sections.

A couple of years ago, I walked into a Verizon store. Since I use T-Mobile, *why'd I do that?* would be a pretty good question. But the better, entrepreneurial question is h*ow?* How did Verizon get me into their store?

The store caught my eye from the street. *How'd they do that?*

It looked inviting. *How'd they do that?*

I don't know. It was colorful and bright and friendly. *How'd they do that?*

Standing in the store, I took another look around. It really was bright. I glanced up at the ceiling and noticed the lights. They didn't look like ordinary showroom lights, they were set at an unusual angle, and they somehow made everything look clean and energetic. When I went back to my store, it seemed really gloomy in comparison, which it never had before. I asked my staff. They thought we were fine, no one ever complained that they couldn't see our products, and the room got a ton of natural light, but it wasn't Verizon.

I went back. I talked to the people who worked there, took a photo of the lights, went online, and ordered them. My electrician installed them, and they looked great. But I'd noticed more than the lights. Test yourself here—what else was different? I went up the ladder and fiddled around until I got them angled just right.

The showroom looks great now. No one had noticed a problem, but they did notice how much better it looked after we got the new lights hung, and now, sometimes people walk into the store, and I can see them looking around a little confused. They don't wear hair extensions; they just walked in off the street, and they're thinking, *Why'd I do that?*

RESEARCH

The first step in getting curious is noticing when somebody is doing something different or when you have a different reaction to something than you usually do. I noticed I was responding differently to the Verizon store than I do to most storefronts. I'll notice when I click on an ad instead of ignoring it. You have to be receptive to notice things. If you're too involved in your own thinking or if you're on autopilot, you'll miss a lot.

Make a habit of noticing.

The second step is noticing on purpose. When you're looking for something, you're doing more than just letting it catch your eye. Instead of waiting for things to capture your attention, turn your attention to finding things to be curious about. This is research. For people in the hair business, research means setting aside time to get out into the world and to go online and to deliberately go looking for showrooms, businesses, blogs, and YouTube channels that are doing something interesting. Study them from a business perspective. Be analytical. Visit other people's websites and look at the technology they're using. If you put something in the shopping cart and leave the site, do you get reminders later that you left something there? *How'd they do that?*

I spend time talking to employees when I'm in stores. I ask how business is going, about the local market, about what kind of advertising or promotions they've got going on. It's amazing how much you can learn about a business—even a competitor—from just chatting with the people who work there.

It can be trickier to research a company from the top down. CEOs are hard to get in touch with, many of them aren't on social media, and they tend to safeguard their time. That doesn't mean you can't get the questions you'd like to ask answered, even by someone famous and seemingly unreachable. Many of them have written books—go read them! Of those who haven't, most have done interviews online or on podcasts (you could start with Hair Biz Radio, a podcast I co-host.) If you see a company that's doing something you like, and you want to research how they've done it, Google who the CEO is and then search for that person's name and the word "interview." You can almost always find something worthwhile.

Online interviews and podcasts let you learn from the masters without paying the kind of entry fee or tuition it'd take to hear them speak as a guest lecturer in business schools or at conferences. As a bonus, if you do ever get the chance to talk to someone you admire, being able to reference something they wrote in their book or said on a podcast shows them you're sincere about your interest and gives you a place to start a conversation that's more interesting to them than how cool you think they are.

You can also reach out to prominent people on LinkedIn and Facebook. Your odds of getting an answer aren't great, but there are a few things you can do to increase the likelihood of getting an answer:

- Ask one really specific question that wouldn't take them long to answer. Make sure they haven't already answered that question somewhere public that you could have found on your own with a little research.
- Ask about something they *have* said elsewhere. A follow-up question is more likely to get an answer.
- Ask a one-and-done. Busy people are leery about starting a back-and-forth conversation, but if they think they can help someone out with a quick one-time reply to an interesting and targeted question, particularly one they know they're uniquely qualified to answer, they're more likely to answer you.

But be careful who you ask for advice and even more careful about advice you're given without asking. The internet is full of so-called experts with blogs on marketing, Facebook ads, or pretty much any other topic you can think of. When your research turns up this kind of advice, take a minute to qualify the person giving it.

Are they successful? Is their advice based on their own experience or on some theory they've made up? Have their recommendations worked for other people? There are five thousand companies on the Inc. 5,000 list. It's not luck that got them there. People with companies on the high end of that list are doing something right. Companies that move up the list quickly or companies in your industry are a great place to start your research.

RECORDING

Write down what you observe and your analysis of it. Collect it all in your notebook so you can go back later—maybe even years later—and revisit it. You may see a store display or an online tool now that you're not ready to implement, but later, when you're in a position to use it, all you'll remember is that you saw something cool related to what you're ready to start. This can be extraordinarily frustrating if the only way you have of retrieving it is combing your memories. It's much easier to go re-read your notebook. You might even pick up some cool ideas you didn't remember you'd had!

PRO TIP: YOUR NOTEBOOK

It can be very hard to maintain awareness when you're online. There are so many distractions! Pop-ups and notifications and endless links to follow until you end up somewhere you had no intention of going. Going old school with a paper notebook and a pen can do a lot to keep you focused. You won't be able to organize everything on paper the way you can digitally, but I think it's worth the trade-off not to keep your notes and lists on your phone. Sure, if you don't have your notebook with you, you can use your phone to take a picture or send yourself a note, but once you get back to your notebook, transfer everything to paper. That way, everything related to your business will be in one place, and even if it isn't as searchable, the process of looking through it isn't wasted at all. In fact, I think it's part of the value!

EXPERIENCE

Get curious about your own experiences. Learning to ask *how* about both your successes and failures, your strengths and weaknesses, your good days and bad helps you find out what works for you and what doesn't. In the same way, you want to take a business perspective on how other companies do what they do, observe, and analyze yourself. Look for what works, record it in your notebook, and then do more of that.

In 2018, I hired one of the top website SEO teams in the world who told me I needed to increase the number of articles I posted to our website. I remember feeling proud of myself on my next check-in, able to report I'd published twenty full-length articles in the last month. He said the consultant equivalent of, "That's nice, dear," and I asked what it would take to impress him. He told me if I wanted to be the number one company on the web, I needed to write a hundred articles a month. *That's impossible!*

At least it is until you start asking how. How could I publish a 1,500-plus word article every business day? The difference between "Can I do it?" and "How can I do it?" makes all the difference. The answer to the first is easy: No. The answer to the second ended up being: hire a team of thirty freelance writers and a full-time editor. We did one hundred 2,000-word blog posts every month for eight months.

GET FEEDBACK

While you're working to get thinking, getting other people's thoughts is almost like getting a shortcut. Feedback increases the number of minds working on your business and gives you a perspective you can't get on your own. Trying to be objective about your business is like trying to see your own face with no mirror. You need business feedback for the same reason—it's impossible for you to see your business accurately because you're seeing it from the inside. You'll need outside eyes—at least four of them, one set to wear the rose-colored glasses and another with no filter at all.

POSITIVE FEEDBACK

Sales are the only feedback you can believe absolutely, but everyone needs a cheerleader. Starting a business is hard, and you're going to get discouraged. Remembering your *why* will help, but when you're so low down you can't see something lofty, you need at least one person who thinks what you're doing is great and who will cheer you up and on.

CRITICAL FEEDBACK

Honest, clear-eyed feedback is almost impossible to get from anyone who loves you. It's not easy to find someone who's willing to tell you yes, your company looks fat in those jeans (or unprofessional in that color scheme). But without that kind of feedback, your business will go out into the world, not looking its best. People won't be attracted to it, you won't steadily pick up more sales, and—worst of all—you'll never understand why.

Finding Critical Feedback

The first step in finding a solid source of objective feedback about your company is to recognize you need it. The second step is to acknowledge it might be painful to hear. You're not looking for people who want to hurt your feelings, but you want people who will tell the truth even if it does. If their intention is constructive, your feelings are yours to handle. Step three is to look outside your immediate network.

> Small failures lead to big wins.

Over the years, I've noticed that an ability to accept critical feedback either from other people or directly from failure itself is a hallmark trait of successful entrepreneurs.

WHEN TO GET FEEDBACK

Before you launch your business, and after you've had a disappointing setback, are the best times to seek critical feedback. Getting an outside opinion about your brand design, your website, a new marketing strategy, or additional product lines before you commit weeks or months of time and any amount of money just makes good business sense. If other people have had a bad experience with a vendor or lost money on a new kind of advertising, getting their opinion of your plan can save you a tremendous amount of time, money, and heartbreak. Early feedback while you're still in the planning stages or after you've executed and before you've launched is a great remedy to the dangerous kind of over-confidence that seems to be part of the hasn't-failed-yet entrepreneur.

PRO TIP: FACEBOOK GROUPS

Our Facebook group (https://hairbiz.tips/group) is full of smart, generous people who can be an incredible source of useful feedback on everything from logo design to pricing products, but Facebook has hundreds of groups for entrepreneurs, and you'll find resources by joining several that seem like a good fit for your particular needs and situation.

When something you've tried hasn't worked as well as you expected, taking a step back and asking yourself *how'd that happen?* is the place to start looking for the cause. Asking for an unbiased outside opinion is an even better one. Here, the effect on confidence is often the reverse of what it was in the planning phase. A person who isn't emotionally involved can often see what's working as well as what isn't. If you're 90 percent of the way there, having someone point out what's missing can keep you from throwing away time and work that could easily be salvaged or pivoted in a new direction.

As your business grows, your problems grow with it. Having positive feedback to cheer you on and reliable sources of critical feedback to help you stay (or get back) on course allows you to keep going and keep growing. Entrepreneurs need to be optimistic, but expecting the best can make failure more damaging to ego (and operations) than it has to be. Feedback helps temper your optimism and lighten your darker days.

BE FEARLESS

Fear kills more companies than anything else, and it keeps even more from ever getting started in the first place. Fear keeps you from doing the things you need to do, and it's the single biggest impediment to learning. No one wants to look foolish or dumb, and that's always a risk when you're trying something new. It's safer not to try.

Your business is more important than your embarrassment.

I still have to remind myself of this lesson. Right now, I'm learning Mandarin Chinese. Because I've learned to double up on things to get more done in a day, I practice while I'm on the Atlanta Belt-Line—a beautiful walking path through the city. So if you're ever there and see a tall white guy muttering to himself in Mandarin, wave. It's probably me. (Even if it's not, it's nice to be friendly.)

When I first started taking my foreign language tapes on my evening walks, I worried about what people were thinking about me. I could have let that worry inhibit me and given up on my walk or my Mandarin, but worry is just another word for fear, and I've decided not to be afraid of thoughts in other people's heads. I have enough of my own.

Learning not to worry about what other people think can be a little trickier when they're the people closest to you, and their thoughts come out of their mouths. It's still disappointing, if no longer surprising, to me how often I hear stories from people getting started in the hair business who shared their dreams with a family member or friend and got negative comments, mockery, or even sabotage in return.

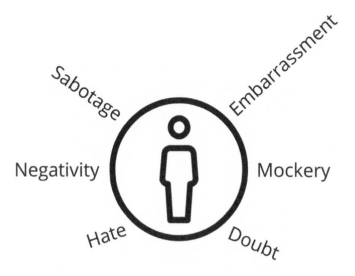

I think some people find any kind of change threatening, and family and friends particularly can worry that your new business will take some of your time and attention from them. (It will.) Some people will be prompted by jealousy to be negative about your exciting new venture. Some people are just mean. Protect your new business from anyone who turns a firehose on your parade.

In my experience, the more successful you become, the fewer old friends you have. Not everyone you know will handle your success gracefully, but those who do, who cheer you on, celebrate your wins with you, and encourage you when you're down will be your friends for life!

Of course, worrying about looking bad in front of strangers or friends is only one flavor of the fear that can stop an entrepreneur. There's also fear of failure, fear of success, fear of rejection, fear of disappointment—there's a whole Baskin Robbins of fear, and fudge sauce is only occasionally the answer. I have two other responses that I've found work well for me.

CALL IT OUT

I stopped worrying about whether or not I should take my Chinese on my walks once I realized that fear was what was holding me back. Fear is sneaky. It almost never shows up in your mind telling the truth. Instead, it says things like:

- I'm too busy.
- I'm too tired.
- I don't have the money.
- I don't have the time.
- I don't know what to do.
- I don't know how to do it.

Sure, sometimes you *are* too busy, but if you had time to do something less important, chances are it's fear that's stopping you. Getting a business up and running is hard enough without fear holding you back. Any time you realize there's something you need to do that stays on your to-do list, try to figure out if fear is blocking your forward movement. Sometimes, just acknowledging that what you need to do is a little bit scary is enough to get you over the fear and into action. Learn to recognize fear for what it is and call it by its name. Sometimes, simply saying, "That's just fear talking" is all it takes to beat it.

ACCEPT IT

Whatever you're afraid of will happen. Not because you're afraid of it, but because pretty much anything that can happen in entrepreneurship will. You will fail, you will succeed, you will sacrifice things, you will make mistakes.

You will fail frequently and with varying degrees of grace. If you fail to fail, you're failing to try. Get used to it. Once you've screwed up a couple things a couple of times, you learn that failure isn't fatal, and it gets a little less scary. Do the thing that scares you and when you succeed, celebrate the win. When you fail, dust yourself off and celebrate the getting back up.

You will succeed, and things will change. People may treat you differently, and you may feel unworthy of the good things you get. The good news here is that (no matter what you see on Instagram), success never blows up overnight. You'll have time to practice handling it. Just like you learn to get up and keep going after a fall, you learn to come back down to earth and go back to work after a win. Being an entrepreneur is about the work, not the successes or the failures. You set goals, but they're signposts along the way. There is no destination, and you never really arrive.

All fears are like the two biggies (of winning and losing), and you can learn to embrace whatever you're afraid of the same way. Recognize that having the experience won't kill you. (Unless it legitimately might, in which case, stay afraid *and away!*) And when something you've been afraid of happens, remember:

- You'll get through this—you've gotten through everything that's come before it, haven't you?
- Every experience teaches you how to handle it better and fear it less.
- Every time something you've feared happens, you'll get to feel proud of yourself on the other side.
- Fear is only a problem if you let it stop you. Learn to welcome it as the old friend it is—one that only shows up when something important is going down. You're scared because you care.

Really getting your arms around fear is a little like the first time you break up with somebody. When you're sixteen, and your first relationship ends, you think your whole life is going down in flames and taking all love and joy with it forever. But after you've had a few relationships and survived a few break-ups, you know the shape of the pain, and you learn to recognize the warning signs. Maybe you learn to get out of relationships a little earlier rather than letting the fear of the break-up keep you stuck. You get better at the actual endings, and you know that after the sad days and lonely nights, things start to get better.

DESTROY IT

When you procrastinate or ignore things you need to do or issues you need to think about, they don't go away just because you're not looking at them. You can shove them to the back of your mind, but on some level, you still feel them there like monsters under the bed. You might not be able to identify the cause of the growling, scratchy anxiety you feel, but a really cool thing happens when you drag the scary tasks and thoughts out into the light and slash them off your to-do list—you get a little jolt of relief or even victory. Get addicted to it.

Learn to look for and crave the little thrill that lives just on the other side of doing something you've been resisting. Your peace of mind and your self-respect get dragged down by the weight of undone tasks, and every one you eliminated lets it rise a little higher.

It's another part of being a mental athlete. You get the same kind of endorphin rush runners get by pushing through the physical discomfort. There's a doer's high, and once you get hooked, nothing can stop you.

REFRAME IT

One of the best ways I know of handling fear, particularly fear of failure is to stop needing to handle it because you've stopped being afraid.

Failure is feedback.

Feedback is so important that we've already had a whole section on it in the last chapter. Failure is simply information coming back that something didn't work. Life is an ongoing series of experiments. Failure answers one test with, "Nope!" Take the information and try something else. Looking at failure as feedback can take the emotional sting out of it. It can also keep you from making the same mistake again.

Here, too, the entrepreneur's question is helpful. When something goes wrong, instead of asking, *Why is this happening to me?* try, *How'd that happen?*

Be really honest with yourself when you ask that question. In my experience, the most common *hows* of failure are: I wasn't consistent, I didn't put in the time, and I misjudged the audience. Fear is usually the *why* behind all those *hows,* so, well, rinse and repeat.

If starting and running a business is something you love doing (and stop right now if it isn't!), the education you get from doing it, no matter the outcome, is worth more than any amount of time and money you may have "lost." Think of it as your tuition at the very best school there is—Experience U.

Every false step is still a step closer to finding a path that will eventually get you where you want to go.

YOUR TURN: GET THINKING

Get your notebook! The habits of asking the entrepreneurial *how*, of getting and taking feedback, and of learning to handle fear require practice, and thinking skills (weirdly) can only be practiced by doing things, not thinking about them.

BE CURIOUS

I don't know many women who can go into a Sephora and not come out with one of those cute stripy bags. *How'd they do that?*

Observe and Analyze

Go to Sephora. Look around. Notice how bright the store is, the nice packaging on display, the music they're playing, the staff all in their black smocks. Don't buy anything. You're saving money to start your business. Besides, you're not shopping now, you're looking—practice thinking like a business owner, not a customer.

Go to the grocery store. Notice all the little impulse purchase items on display in the check-out line and how easy it is to just toss one into your cart. Notice how they've used the ends of the aisles. Notice how you have to walk a long way from the entrance to get to the milk. How many people go to the store because they need to pick up a half-gallon for their breakfast? How many other things do you think they pick up as they pass them on the way back there?

The big chain stores and the big products they carry spend millions of dollars tweaking the shopping experience, and they've done such a good job most people have no idea what's going on. Unless you have a real investigator's mentality, you're just going to wonder why it's so hard to get out of Target for under $100. *How'd they do that?*

Steal their ideas. Let them spend their millions doing research on customer behavior and store layout. Notice it, analyze, record it, and use it yourself.

Research

Pick two stores or two brands in the same niche that are about the same size—two local barbers or Mexican restaurants or liquor stores—one popular and one not. Visit both. Ask yourself what they're doing differently. There will probably be hundreds of answers. Try to analyze which aspects have the biggest impact.

Go to a popular e-commerce site every other day for a week. The first day, look around a little, click on a couple of products, then leave. Notice, over the next forty-eight hours, the ads that show up on your Facebook and Instagram feeds. Two days later, go back to the site and add something to your cart. Go to the check-out page, but don't check out. What changes in the ads do you see over the next forty-eight hours? My bet is that you'll see a different set of ads with a different level of call-to-action. The best companies are doing extremely detailed targeting. *How'd they do that?* (The answer is the Facebook Pixel—for my money, the single most powerful paid marketing platform ever. I'll teach you how to use it in chapter 6, but awareness of it and experience with it now will give you an advantage.)

Record

In your notebook, write down what you noticed at Sephora and the grocery store. Take notes on your analysis of the popular and less-popular businesses in the same niche. Track your experience with the e-commerce site's targeted ads. Being familiar with these tools and ideas from the user's point of view before you start implementing them yourself will help you be more creative.

Write down all the ideas you can steal. You won't be using the same ads the big e-commerce sites use, but you can create something with a similar flow that really targets your customer base. Notice what kinds of marketing messages grab your attention.

BUILD YOUR PERSONAL BOARD OF DIRECTORS

Think about the people you know. Who are the cheerleaders? Who can you count on to pick you back up when you get knocked down? Would any of the people you know be willing and able to give you critical feedback, even if it upset you? Where else can you get that kind of support?

BE FEARLESS

Look back at your to-do list for the last week and circle the most important thing you didn't get done. If you don't have a to-do list for the last week, write down "use a to-do list" and circle that.

Ask yourself what fear kept you from doing what you circled. Don't accept any excuses. It was important, and you didn't do it. Why not?

Get curious. There's no shame here. You're not bad or wrong or stupid. Something's stopping you. What is it? Try to be as scientific as you can. If you can't figure it out, ask someone you trust and who knows you well. Remember, other people have a better view of you than you can from inside your own skull. Ask them what fear they think might be getting in your way of doing what you need to do to get what you want.

Name your fear. Write it down. Remember your *why*.

Examples:

- My fear of success thwarts my efforts to own my own house.
- My fear of being humiliated distracts me from creating a better life for myself and my kids.
- My fear of failure limits my ability to help women feel beautiful.
- My fear of rejection blocks me from being a great example for my sister.

Accept it. Absolutely every person on the planet is afraid. Fear is a good and useful thing, and it's baked into us as human beings.

Write your fear down in your notebook: *I'm afraid of success, I'm afraid of humiliation, I'm afraid of failure, I'm afraid of rejection.*

Now write down one thing you're going to do in spite of that fear. Maybe it's the thing you circled, maybe it's something even riskier that triggers the same fear.

Commit to doing it. Get in touch with your why, set a goal, make it realistic, and make a plan. Then do it. Do it right now.* Feel the rush? Get hooked on it.

*If you can't do it right now, schedule it. If you don't do it right now (or at the time you scheduled), break it down into smaller and smaller pieces until you find one that sneaks in under the fear radar, and do that.

Sometimes, the thing you're afraid of happens. That's okay, too. If you've been putting off calling someone you need to talk to because you're afraid they're going to reject you, most of the time, they won't. It's just the fear that's been stopping you. But when your fear is proven right—and sometimes it will be—it's not any fun. Remember, failure is feedback. Maybe that person is just someone you need to stop dealing with. Ask them why they rejected you; maybe you need to up your game and try again. The only real failure is failure to try again.

NOW YOU'RE THINKING!

As Yogi Berra once said of baseball, entrepreneurship is "Ninety percent mental. The other half is physical." In the first chapter, I gave you a list of what to expect; in this chapter, I've tried to help you start to think about your thinking. The habits of asking *how,* of getting feedback and being fearless are pretty personal, and I've stepped outside what traditional business books think is important to teach aspiring entrepreneurs, but the three skills in this chapter are at the very core of my success.

I've written this chapter for you because it's the chapter I needed most when I was starting out. Yes, it's personal. I'm climbing right inside your head and telling you how to think. If you already knew this stuff, I hope you don't mind the reinforcement, but if thinking *how,* actively looking for people to tell you hard truths, and handling fear by calling it out, accepting it, destroying it, and reframing it aren't skills that come naturally to you, once you start, you'll be way ahead of where I was when I was first starting out.

Being curious teaches you to find solutions by asking *how*, by looking for *what worked*, and to answer failure with *why?* Being curious points you in the right direction.

Being critiqued regularly is how you keep from getting off course. You simply can't get an accurate picture of your business from inside it, and an inaccurate picture can run you into a wall.

Being fearless makes you unstoppable.

While curiosity sets you in the right direction and feedback holds you on course, courage keeps you moving forward. As you start picking up speed, you'll need to start internalizing what you learn—and that's what education is all about.

CHAPTER 3

GET EDUCATED

I was twenty-nine and had built CurrySimple to the point where it was successful and exciting enough that the Washington Post was interviewing me about it. I can still remember the time of day, the angle of the sun, and the fact that I was doing the interview in my car, although I can't remember why. It wasn't the first time I'd spoken with the interviewer Michaele Weissman—we were wrapping things up, getting a few extra details when she said something to me, just casually in passing, that changed the way I understood myself. I don't remember what I'd just said, but I'll always remember her response. "Sure," she said. "That makes sense. You know you have a couple of learning disabilities, right?"

No. No, I did not know that.

I guess she didn't notice my shocked silence—I'm not typically the quiet kind—because she went on to say it was something she saw a lot in the entrepreneurs she interviewed—ADHD and terrible handwriting and a mind that jumped around from topic to big idea, to detail, to random observation, to joke. I'll admit it—at the time, I wasn't just surprised, I was offended. Today, I'm incredibly grateful. No one likes hearing there's something wrong with them—the second "D" in ADHD stands for "disorder," and I didn't feel disordered. I was a businessman, and a successful one, thank you very much. But she was right.

She was right about a couple of things. I did (and do) have more than one learning D-for-differences. I don't learn the way other people do. I struggled the whole way through my education. I don't think I ever finished a book until I was in my thirties. Finding out the reason why let me take another look at my past, understand it better, and do things differently going forward.

The reporter was also right that many entrepreneurs have the same kind of not-the-same. Not all entrepreneurs have ADHD; some have other learning differences, mental health issues, or emotional peculiarities. Turns out, people who think differently are the same people who can create something different, something new, like their own companies.

I'd always felt like figuring things out and getting things done was harder for me than for "normal" people. But in the years since that reporter shook up my idea of myself, I've worked with a lot of aspiring and successful entrepreneurs, and I've seen what she meant. A lot of what is weird about me is pretty normal in the large population of talented, intelligent people who itch to create something new of their own and who, like me, are able to make more rapid progress once they understand their own differences.

LEARN HOW TO LEARN

I haven't spent a couple hours talking to you, so I can't just rattle off a list of your learning disabilities (differences) the way that reporter did for me, but don't wait to be interviewed by the

Washington Post to figure this stuff out for yourself. If I had understood earlier why I sometimes couldn't understand material as it was presented, I would have become more successful more quickly, and with a lot less shame. Maybe you want to go get yourself tested, but I never did. For me, the simple awareness was enough for me to start making some changes that made a big difference in my life.

AWARENESS

You can't fix problems you don't know you have. Bringing the same kind of heightened awareness we talked about taking into stores and showrooms and onto internet sites in the last chapter, when turned on yourself, can show you where you may be having a harder time than other people. Try to keep the same kind of non-judgmental observational mindset and just notice. Do you forget things other people seem able to remember? Do you feel like information that just sinks in for some bounces off you? Does it feel impossible for you to focus on anything longer than a minute? Can you absolutely not do math? Does it just take you longer to master something that seems to come easily to other people? Do you hate, hate, hate doing something other people do for fun? As an entrepreneur, a lot of your success is going to depend on how quickly you can learn certain kinds of things. Once you know what's not working, you can start finding workarounds, ways to play to your strengths, tools that prop you up, and tricks that make things easier for you.

ACCEPTANCE

The first big change I made was letting myself off the hook. I stopped beating myself up about what I thought I couldn't do. I discovered that I could learn and learn well, just not the same way other people do.

It's not that you can't. You can. The trick is figuring out *how* you can.

Once you get past the "I can't" and start asking that entrepreneurial *how* question, you'll be amazed at how much you thought was out of reach has been right there at your fingertips. Or maybe, it's been right there at the tips of your toes, once you start using your feet instead of your hands. (Before I get totally lost in body parts, really, it's more likely to be ears—listening to audiobooks or podcasts instead of reading, or hands-on trying things for yourself.) But until you can accept these things about yourself, you can't move on to the next stage of learning what's going on and harnessing the true power of your intelligence. Because you *are* smart. It just looks different on you than it does on other folks. Spiderman had to get bitten by a spider, and then he had to go in for some serious training before he could swing between buildings by a thread. And he still can't do what Aquaman can. If you're a Spiderman trying to swim, get out of the water!

ASSESSMENT

There are doctors and specialists who can run tests and give diagnoses, but you can probably do a lot of that evaluation yourself. Try to look carefully at where you're struggling and be as specific as you can about what's hard for you. Then flip it around and look for what's easy. Stop thinking about learning as something that only happens in school. I never did well in math, but I really like numbers, and I'm good at accounting—it just comes naturally to me. What comes naturally to you? What do other people ask you for advice about or help with? What do you like doing?

Look at the things you're good at and ask yourself how you learned to do them. Unless it's breathing, crying, or burping, it is something you learned how to do. *How'd you do that?* Is it something you took apart or broke and then figured out how to fix? Is it something you watched someone else do and copied until you could do it on your own? Get curious about it.

I asked a friend of mine who's a teacher about the different ways people learn, and she said there were primarily three paths: audio, visual, and audio-visual. There are people who can hear information—from lectures or audiobooks or conversations—and pick it up just from listening or from listening and talking about it. Other people need to see things—words or pictures, diagrams, or infographics—before they can internalize the information. Still other people (including me) learn best only when they have both. I'm a proud graduate of YouTube University, and I'm not alone! If you learn best by hearing someone explain what they're doing while you watch a video of them doing it, you're never going to get as much out of just hearing it or looking at pictures.

Figure out for yourself how you can consume the most information the most quickly.

Once you've figured out where you do well and where you struggle, look for ways to use the one to fix the other. If you learn really well working one-on-one, find someone to teach you. If you can only focus for a short period of time, schedule yourself to do a little bit over a lot of short sessions.

Do you learn better at a desk or on the sofa, at a coffee shop, or in a classroom? Are you more likely to get stuff done in a single, intense, all-day session or a little bit every day? Do you do better when there's a schedule you have to follow or a class that starts at a specific time and place, so you know that if you're not there, you'll miss it, or do you get more done when you can be flexible about when you do it?

Everyone learns differently. There's no standard and no "right way." The only wrong way is not to figure out your way. There's a lot of research about learning styles and differences online. There are tricks and tips for coping with different issues and blogs about people who have figured out ways of dealing with almost anything. It might take a little bit of time to figure out what you need and how to help yourself do more and better, but you'll be at an enormous competitive advantage if you put in the work to learn how to work better. Most people never take the time and leave a huge advantage on the table. Most people, even most entrepreneurs, never really dig into what their superpowers are. Don't be a swimming Spiderman!

PRACTICE EVERY DAY

Everyone expects to have to practice their jump shot or their backflip. Athletes are athletes because they train. You are a mental athlete. Practice. Over and over. Every day. Keep focused on getting stronger and better. Expect bad days and set-backs, but try to look at even that as practice. Practice getting back up when you trip. Practice going back the next day. You're learning how to coach yourself at the same time you're learning how to play. Practice all of it.

LEARN HOW TO TWEAK

Entrepreneurs learn constantly. Every day you work on your business, you're going to learn something new. Sometimes, you'll be learning by doing, and sometimes you'll hit a wall and have to go learn how to do whatever it is you need to do next. If you've been playing along with the Your Turn challenges at the end of each chapter, you will have already learned about having a why and about the entrepreneurial *how*. As we keep going, you'll learn how to set up an LLC and the basics of marketing. Once you launch your business, you'll have to learn even more ever faster. And that's exactly the way it should be. For the next two years particularly, a lot of what you need to learn will be staring you right in the face, or you'll trip over it. Still, there's another kind of learning that can help put you ahead of the pack. The trick is to go looking for it.

> What do you do every day? How could you do it better?

I'm constantly looking for things to tweak—for little ways of leveling up. My most recent life upgrade relates to the amount of business I do overseas. I send a lot of international wire transfers. This requires going to the bank (about a half an hour round trip), waiting in line, and then having someone at the bank actually put the transfer order in. It's a hassle, it's something I have to do several times a week, and it costs $45 per transfer. Not only that, as our company keeps growing, we get closer and closer to hitting the bank's limit for how much we can send overseas in a day. It hasn't happened yet, and it isn't an emergency, but it was a situation that was ripe for a tweak.

I spent most of an afternoon looking for a better solution and discovered American Express has a great international wire system online with only a $25 wire transfer fee. Now, a task that used to take me half an hour takes a minute. That may not seem like a big enough deal to justify the time it took to set it up, but it saves me at least two hours and $100 a week. Every week. That's over $5,000 a year every year for the rest of the time we're in business!

It will also save me a hundred hours or a full week and a half of work if you figure I work an eighty-hour week. Not bad for an afternoon on the internet!

What little tasks do you do every day or every week that, if you could do them more quickly or more cheaply, would save you significant amounts of time and money? What tasks do you hate doing that, if you could do it differently (or not at all), would use up less of your energy and good mood? Look for ways to be more efficient. Are there tasks you can double up on? (Combining education and exercise is one of my favorites.) Time and money are the key factors in your success as an entrepreneur. You'll have more of both to spend on your business if you tweak the efficiency of anything in your life. Save ten minutes a day, and you've added an extra hour to your week. Cut out one half-hour of TV a day, and you've given yourself an entire extra workday every other week.

As an example, let's say your typing speed is on the high side of average—forty words-per-minute—and you spend half an hour a day answering email. If you spend five minutes a day working on an online typing class, you can quickly increase your speed to sixty or even eighty words per minute. That would knock the time you spend on email down by up to a half and free up at least an extra hour a week. Isn't five minutes a day for the next month worth an extra two days every year? You're going to be typing pretty much every day for most of the rest of your life, might as well get good at it!

Small, incremental changes made every day have a bigger impact than big, one-time hard pushes.

LEARN TO BE PROFESSIONAL

People sometimes confuse being emotional with being passionate, but they're not the same. Passion is a tremendous source of energy. It comes from your *why*, and it keeps you moving forward when things go wrong. Emotions are what pull you off course. If you get too angry about a bad review or bummed about your sales numbers, or frustrated with your bookkeeping, you'll send a flaming reply, spend too much on advertising or make an expensive mistake. Keep your feelings out of your business.

Have passion. Be professional.

The stereotype of the ice-cold businesswoman with her hair raked back tight enough to pop out her eyes exists for a reason. You don't have to be uptight, but you do need to think through your business decisions instead of feeling your way through them. The actual work of running a business is mostly problem-solving. You've already learned to expect problems, so they won't surprise you (or they will, but you'll remember you knew they were coming and recover faster), but solving them is better done from a mental place than an emotional one. Just that—the ability to move quickly from feeling into thinking about how to solve a problem—will put you well ahead of many new entrepreneurs.

As I mentioned in chapter 1, because my experience with the 2008 financial crisis taught me to see and pay attention to dark clouds on the business horizon, the business impacts of the coronavirus didn't take me by surprise. I sat my team down and told them some serious craziness was coming and that we needed to prepare for the worst. We didn't freak out, we made a plan, and that plan has allowed us to have our best quarter yet during the outbreak and in the summer, traditionally our slowest time.

BREATHE

Learning to manage your negative emotions and refusing to let them push you into reacting is a huge part of becoming more professional, but feeling good can be a problem, too. Entrepreneurs tend to be optimistic by nature. After all, if we didn't really believe great things can (and probably will) happen, we wouldn't start all this craziness in the first place.

Think of your optimism as a Lamborghini. Just because it can go two hundred miles an hour doesn't mean it should. Keep your optimism throttled back. Don't let it make your decisions any more than you'd give anger the wheel.

> Decide. Don't React.

Your optimism will tell you that it'll all work out—you don't have to stay up late and do all the boring things. It will encourage you to throw money at problems and spend more than you can afford to because you'll make it all back soon. It will urge you to go fast. Don't listen! Go slow. Go deliberate. Go frugal. Go all those boring things that your optimism and excitement don't have time for. You need your optimism like you need your fear, but you have to protect it from itself, too. Don't let fear hit the brakes. Don't let optimism floor the gas.

LEARN TO MANAGE YOUR ENERGY

No one, no matter how inspired, has limitless physical or mental energy. Even more than money, your ability to spend and renew these resources wisely will determine your success as an entrepreneur. Your business will take everything you've got to give and ask for more. If you don't learn to ration your energy, it'll bleed you dry, and you'll quit (or break) before you get where you want to go. Not only that, but pushing on when you're running on fumes will undermine everything else you've accomplished. It's hard to be curious when you're exhausted. It's almost impossible to be rational when you're hungry.

Learn to monitor your energy. It doesn't stay constant throughout the day. Some people jump out of bed going sixty miles an hour. Some people go zero to sixty in an hour and a half. Most people hit a mid-afternoon slump. Some people are at their best after everyone else goes to bed. Figure out the times of day when you're most focused and do your most brain-taxing work then.

Most successful entrepreneurs get into the habit of waking up early and scheduling the most important or most difficult task first thing, although what "early" and "first thing" means can differ by a couple of hours. My business partner, on the other hand, is a night owl. He often starts a project in the hour or two before midnight and puts in four hours before going to bed. I'll get up at four some mornings to tackle the same kind of thing. For both of us, I think it's the quiet and the lack of other people around that make those very late or very early hours so productive. Experiment and figure out what's best for you.

Learn which tasks pump you up and which drain you. If you're extroverted, doing people-oriented tasks when your energy is low might get you going again. If you're introverted, try doing the solo work that you enjoy at those times and save the less comfortable public-facing jobs for times when you feel most alert. It'll take you twice as long to do the things that are hard for you when you're low-energy, but you can often maintain your normal speed at easier ones.

Guard your focus like a pile of cash on your desk. Imagine that every pop-up, every text, each interruption, and all distractions are taking a bill off the stack. We literally *pay* attention. Don't let anything steal yours, and don't give it away.

Your brain is part of your body. That may sound obvious, but it took me a while to figure it out. Your attention and mental energy come from your physical energy, and they slow down before it does. Luckily, they bounce back just as quickly, so anything you do to take care of your body increases your brainpower.

Sleep makes you smarter. So do healthy eating and getting enough exercise. When I eat better, I have more energy to put into my business. Feeding yourself better feeds your business more. Taking time away from your business to go on a walk isn't really taking time away from your business.

Take a walk every day.

I strongly recommend getting into the habit of taking a daily walk. Exercise increases your energy, and a change of scenery can change your mood. Starting a business is stressful, and walks are a great stress-reliever. Bonus points if you listen to a podcast or audiobook on your walk.

LEARN TO BE ORGANIZED

Being disorganized saps your energy and makes everything take more time. It makes learning harder. It interferes with your ability to make the little tweaks and improvements that add up over time. You're more likely to get angry or frustrated if you feel out of control of your time and your stuff, and chaos in those areas amplifies all other fears.

Start experimenting with different organizational systems today. Try out free apps like Google Calendar, Todosit, and Momentum, or buy a daily or weekly paper planner. It really doesn't matter whether you use a digital or a paper calendar, but get used to using one, then make it a habit to check in with it several times a day every day. Decide how you're going to organize your time and how you're going to remember what you decide.

Write down everything!

You can use your notebook or your computer, sticky notes, or your phone, but trust me on this. Don't keep anything in your head that you can write down.

LEARN TO BE CONSISTENT

When I list the *hows* behind most entrepreneurial failures, I always put "I wasn't consistent" first. Consistency is entrepreneurship's magic bean. If you're consistent, your business will grow faster than even better-funded ones with flakier people running them. Start building a habit of being consistent now. Your business will need you to be living it by the time you hit chapter 4. As we move forward, I'll point out other places where consistency is extremely important, but I'm introducing it here to give you an overview. I am 100 percent certain that Private Label Extensions is where it is today because we have been consistent day-in and day-out for the last seven years. Celebrating or sick, traveling or tired, motivated or un-, I put my hours in every single day. The tips I've given you for staying organized and physically and mentally healthy will help you push through the tough days, but when it's chaotic and you're sick and depressed, be consistent anyway!

PUBLIC-FACING CONSISTENCY

The best (and maybe the only) way to build a brand is by consistently reminding your customers and your potential customers who you are. You must be visible to be remembered. For the most part, this means posting regularly to social media, but email, text messaging, web push notifications, and making appearances at live events can also help you keep showing up in front of your customers. If you disappear for six months and then show up in someone's inbox, they're much less likely to open your email than if they'd seen a post on social media from you just the day before. Being visible gives people the feeling that they know you. It creates at least the sense of having a relationship if it doesn't actually create the relationship, which, of course, is what we're shooting for. The more relationships you have with customers, the more customers you'll have.

I'm not a celebrity by any means, but I've been building that public-facing relationship within the Facebook group through years of posting almost daily videos. When people meet me in person, they can get a little star-struck. This, of course, doesn't hurt my ego, but it's good for the company and for our customers, too. They're excited to tell me about having followed me online for years and that creates something of a reciprocal bond. It makes our in-person seminars more effective because it's easier to teach people who already feel connected to you and it also helps a lot with sales. Think about it this way—companies pay influencers and celebrities to endorse their products because they recognize the cash value of the relationship those people have with their followers and fans. You can do the same (more on that in chapter 7), but you can also *be* something of an influencer or celebrity yourself by deliberately and consistently building your relationship with your customers.

> You're not just building a business; you're building a brand.

But it's not enough just to show up. You need to deliver consistent quality. If someone clicks on a link to a blog post but finds it's just advertising or isn't interesting or helpful to them, they're less likely to try again. Consistently offering interesting, high-value, useful content brings people back.

Consistency is even more important once someone's made a purchase from you. There will be weeks when you get too busy or too tired to answer email from customers. Answer it anyway. You have to be consistently available to your customers.

> **TOUGH LOVE**
>
> Are you really able to be consistent? Are you committed to being consistent right now?

INTERNAL CONSISTENCY

Consistency is the key to success, and planning is the key to consistency. It's a great policy to always be working a week ahead. If you're writing the blog post in the same week you plan to post it, and something comes up in your business or personal life, you're going to miss your deadline. If you're writing next week's post this week and something comes up, you still have this week's post ready to go because you wrote it last week. You'll have to play catch-up to get back ahead, but that's much better than missing a week. It's better for your customers because they never see the week's slip, and it's better for you because the last thing you want when you're dealing with a crisis is the anxiety of how you're going to get your blog post done. Entrepreneurship is stressful enough. Planning ahead for consistency is one of the best things you can do to take care of yourself.

> **PRO TIP: AUTOMATE CONSISTENCY**
>
> Most social media sites and blogging platforms have a tool that lets you create your content in advance and then post it for you at your chosen time. Take advantage of it!

You can start a successful business with very little money and while working a full-time job, but if you can't be consistent right now, it might not be the right time to start a business. There's no shame in that. Unless you ignore the facts. I know it can be hard to wait. Starting a business is exciting, but starting a business before you're ready gets expensive and depressing all too quickly.

CONSISTENT CONSISTENCY

Being consistent doesn't mean being perfect. You will miss dead-lines and forget things. It happens. Just don't let it happen twice. Missing one weekly blog post isn't great, but it's a blip. Missing two in a row or missing every third one is being consistently inconsistent. Don't do it! Consistency in business is the same as in every other aspect of your life. If you miss going to the gym one day, you can go back the next day and barely notice. Miss a couple of days in a row, and it gets much, much harder to drag yourself back there, and when you do, your workout feels a lot harder.

Business is a process of adding and maintaining. It's a little like gardening. You buy a plant, you stick it in the ground, and it looks great. But if you don't water it and keep it healthy, it'll die. You can't just keep adding new plants. You have to add new things while maintaining the things you already have in place. You'll start with social media before you even launch. When people start commenting on your posts, you'll need to answer their comments *and keep posting.*

Once you have customers, you'll add email marketing and start doing that while you keep replying to comments and making new posts. The same thing happens when you start getting emails from customers or add SMS marketing. The work keeps growing as your business grows. It does get easier with practice, and eventually, you'll be able to hire someone to help you keep up with it all as it keeps growing, but until then, it's better to delay adding something like SMS or email marketing than to allow your social media or customer service responses to become inconsistent.

YOUR TURN: GET EDUCATED

If curiosity is the meta-trait of entrepreneurship, learning is the meta-skill, but not everyone learns the same way. If you're one of the many smart, creative people who don't happen to learn best the way we're taught in school, learning how you learn can be incredibly liberating and empowering. It can make the difference between success and ongoing struggles and frustration as you start to pick up all the other skills and practices you're going to need as an entrepreneur.

LEARN TO LEARN

Start a new page in your notebook and draw a line down the middle. On the left-hand side, write down all the subjects you studied in school that came easily to you and the things you know you do well. Can you draw a cartoon or pick up a melody better or faster than most people you know? Is your make-up always gorgeous? Can you talk to anyone? What do people ask you for your advice or opinions about? Write it down.

On the other half of the page, write down the subjects in school that were hard for you and anything you know you struggle with. Do numbers make no sense to you? Do you forget things or lose stuff or miss appointments? Are you always late? Is your car a mess? When you think of the people you most admire, what can they do that seems out-of-reach to you?

Now, compare the lists. Get curious! Do you notice themes or trends? If you can remember all the lyrics to a song you've only heard twice but have to read the same sentence three times to know what it says, you'll probably learn better by listening than reading. If everything you touch looks gorgeous, but you can never find your keys, you might have a visual learning style but not the world's best organization skills. Write down what you learn about yourself.

If you're interested enough in starting your own business to have gotten three chapters into this book, I'll bet you're creative. I'll bet making things and starting things (even if you don't always finish them) is one of your gifts. Put that gift to work for you. Get creative! Look for ways the things on the left side of your list can help with those on the right. If you're visual, maybe putting pictures of your keys on the key shelf will help you remember to put your keys there. If you do better with listening than reading, start listening to podcasts or downloading audiobooks.

PRO TIP

Audible.com probably has the largest selection of audiobooks anywhere, but most public libraries carry a large selection of the popular business books, inspiring biographies, and even whole college courses in audio format. You may have to put the most recent ones on a waiting list, but there's more than you'll ever have time to listen to already there, and they're all free.

EXTRA-PRO TIP

You can listen to most audio material at 1.5 speed to learn even more even faster!

TWEAK YOUR TASKS

Go back to the list of things you learned about how you learn from the previous exercise. Pick one thing that seems really important or true. Be really honest with yourself here. You can't fix what you won't let yourself see. Write it down, then we'll put some of your new skills to work for you.

Examples:

- I'm late a lot.
- I'm a really great dancer.
- I love beautiful things.
- I learn things best if I can follow along with someone else who's doing them.

Use Your Why

Remember this from chapter 1? Think about your big *why*. How does the one thing you just wrote down tie back to it?

Examples:

- I'm late a lot. My big why is to own my own house. Being late could make it take longer to save enough to buy a house.
- I'm a really great dancer. My big why is to create a better life for myself and my kids. Adding music and movement to my life might make me happier and healthier and give me more energy to build my business.
- I love beautiful things. My big why is to help women feel beautiful. Beauty inspires me. Maybe adding a component of beauty to the things that are hard for me will motivate me.
- I learn things best if I can follow along with someone else who's doing them. My big why is to set a good example

for my kid sister. I'll start watching how-to YouTube videos with her.

Set Goals

Turn what you've just written down into a goal. If you wrote down a strength, look for a weakness you can pair it with. If you picked something from the other side of your page, do the reverse.

Examples:

- I want to be on time for meetings.
- I want to use music and movement to do something about how I lose track of time.
- I want to start using beauty to change the way I forget to write things down.
- I want to start watching how-to YouTube videos with my sister to be an example of educating yourself.

Have Realistic Expectations

Add numbers to your goal and adjust them until the promise you're expecting yourself to fulfill feels like something you can do if you really try.

Examples:

- I will be on time for three meetings next week.
- I will try two experiments on how I might use music and movement to help me keep track of time.
- I will make my notebook beautiful enough that I write things down more and forget less.
- I will watch an hour of how-to YouTube videos with my sister.

Have a Plan

Turn your realistic, why-motivated goal into a plan that will help you tweak something you've learned about how you learn.

Examples:

- Next week, I'm going to be twenty minutes early for the PA meeting, my doctor's appointment, and the meeting I set with myself to work on my business. Once I get there, and while I'm waiting for the meeting to start, I'll reward myself by looking at houses for sale or at home decorating sites, which I won't let myself do any other time.
- I will set the alarm on my phone to play music I love every hour on the hour and see if that helps me keep track of time. I'll listen to fast music that keeps me moving to see if doing that gets me in and out of the grocery store faster and without getting so distracted.
- I'll spend ten minutes decorating my notebook and making it beautiful every day after I write down the things I need to remember.
- I'll call my sister and set up a time for us to watch YouTube tutorials together.

Do whatever you plan to do every day. If you fail to do it consistently, or if what you tried doesn't work, use the opportunity to practice handling failure. Try again. Tweak what you try. Enlist your most encouraging friends to check up on you and cheer you on. Share your experiment with someone you trust and ask for feedback—can they see from the outside where you're making a mistake or missing something that you can't see from inside yourself?

BE PROFESSIONAL

Over the next week, pay attention to when you get emotional. Notice the kind of things that trigger you and what your impulses tell you to do when you're upset. Do you find it very difficult not to respond when someone makes you angry, or do you tend to sink into inactivity? What helps you get back into your calm, businessperson mind when you get disrupted? How does your upset feel? Do your shoulders try to climb into your ears? Does your stomach turn into a fist? Learn to recognize what sets you off, how it feels, and what it makes you want to do. Then make a plan to do something else until you feel calm again. It can be really useful to write rules for yourself.

Examples:

- When I feel like shooting off an angry email, I'll get away from my desk for twenty minutes.
- If I want to crawl back into bed and hide from it all, I'll re-read my whys.
- Whenever I have to deal with the bank, I get freaked out, so I'll do it first thing in the morning when I'm at my best.

MANAGE YOUR ENERGY

For at least three days in a row, set a timer for every two hours and when it goes off, make a quick note of the time and your energy level. Do it consistently! You can use a ten-point scale or a simple plus or minus sign. Track what time you wake up, and when you go to bed. When you're done, look back at your notes and check for patterns. Do you wake up about the same time every day? When are you most energized? Most sluggish? Are you more energetic in the mornings or at night? Do you slow down before mealtime or after you eat? How about caffeine?

Take a good look at last week's to-do list. Notice the tasks that you put off. These may be things that sap your energy or that scare you. Experiment with doing them first thing or whenever else you seem to have the most energy.

Are you eating well and getting enough exercise and sleep? If not, consider using the tweak protocol to adjust whichever of the three seems to have the most impact on your energy levels.

BE ORGANIZED

If you don't already have an organizational system that keeps track of your time and your tasks, experiment with one that appeals to you. If you've learned that you're a visual person, try a paper system like a calendar, datebook, or day planner and a written to-do list. I *love* checking things off a list. Other people like keeping everything on their phones. It can be harder to see a whole week or stretch of months this way, but if you've discovered that digital alerts are lifesavers for you, this might be the way to go. It really doesn't matter what system you use. It matters that you have a system and that you get addicted to using it.

BE CONSISTENT

To practice consistency, I recommend starting to blog now, while you're still early in your entrepreneurial journey. You don't have to have a WordPress blog or even a Facebook account at this point, it's more about building the habit than about creating content, but at least a few of the posts you write while you're building your business may well end up on your company's blog.

Maintaining a blog for your company can be a lot of work, but it's a great way to build relationships with your customers and improve your website's ranking with Google. Since Google is the biggest search engine and can send a lot of potential customers to your site, it's well worth your time to increase your odds this way. And now is a great time to get started (and consistent) with it.

It doesn't really matter when or how you do it, but making a commitment to consistently write one blog post a week is a great way to start creating content, to build excitement in advance of your launch, and to build your consistency muscle. A month from now, if you don't have at least three blog posts written, you may need to revisit the question of whether now is the right time for you to start a business.

Writing Blog Posts

For starters, pick your top three favorite products that you know you want to sell and write a blog post about each of them explaining why you love it and how to use it. Try to write content that makes people excited to see what you'll write next! Your goals for a blog are two-fold: to build your brand's relationship with its customers and to drive traffic. Keeping your posts focused on your products, your business, and your industry will increase the odds that Google will send people your way.

PRO TIP

Don't write about things that aren't related to your business. Your customers aren't interested, and you'll confuse Google.

Blog posts should be a minimum of 1,000 words long, have at least one picture, internal links to products or other blog posts and contain at least two external links to reputable sources that are related to your article. While it's fine to have a couple "My

Journey" posts, remember you want to be interesting. You want to give readers something that makes them want to come back and read your next post. Statistics say e-commerce websites with an active blog sell more products. Be part of the favorable statistic!

Free traffic from Google in the last 12 months

Example

Let's say you're going to write a blog post about how to color hair. As you're writing the instructions, think about ways to include things that will give you a reason to link to other pages on your site and to popular external sites. If you use a Paul Mitchell color, for example, link to its product page on their site but also talk about color and wigs that you'll have on your site so you can add links to them when you start building your site.

Learn more about blogging: https://hairbiz.tips/blogging.

NOW YOU'RE EDUCATED!

I never read a full book in high school. I just couldn't do it. It wasn't until I was almost thirty that I understood why. I have a couple of learning differences, and I'm incredibly easily distracted. Today, I've learned enough about how I learn that, when there's something I need to read, I never try to do it when I'm tired. I'll fall asleep instantly. I never try to read in front of my computer or TV. Instead, I've converted a large closet in my office into my reading room. (I got the idea from George Costanza in a Seinfeld episode.) There's nothing in there but a beanbag chair and a lamp. I go in and sit there when I need to read something, and it works out great!

I leave the door open because I'm not a crazy person, but there aren't any distractions, and I've learned to associate that one place with that one activity I used to dread. Now it's really pretty nice. I won't be going for my Ph.D. any time soon, but when I have reading I must do to learn something I need to know, I can do it because I've educated myself on the conditions I need to learn the way I learn.

By turning the entrepreneurial question of *how* on yourself, you can learn how you learn, overcome any shame you may have around it, capitalize on your strengths, and get some scaffolding around your weaknesses. Once you've educated yourself, it's time to get into action!

CHAPTER 4

GET GOING

There's an old saying, "You have to spend money to make money." It's true. From the minute you take this chapter's second step until you hit your chapter 1 goal of becoming profitable, you're losing money. Make no mistake—this is a race. The faster you can get from here to there, the less you'll have to pay, and the sooner you'll get paid. The six steps in this chapter are in a specific order that helps you get from here to there fast. They are: Product Planning, Market Research, Identity Creation, Business Creation, Budget Revision, and Inventory Ordering. I recommend reading through the whole chapter once first and then doing the steps. Do them in order, do them fast, and you'll be on your way!

STEP 1. PRODUCT PLANNING

What are you selling? Pretty obvious, right? You're selling hair. But what kind of hair? Wigs, extensions, or both? What else are you selling?

STEP 1.A. WHAT YOU'LL SELL

It can be really tempting to set up an online store that sells everything you like. Don't do it! A hair and boot store will be really hard to market. In the beginning, start with things that make sense together. You can always add other product lines later on. On the other hand, if your company only sells wigs while another company sells wigs and the lace glue that goes with the wigs, customers might pick your competitor just because they're more of a one-stop shop.

STEP 1.B. WHERE YOU'LL GET IT/HOW YOU'LL DELIVER IT

Where you get your products will depend on several factors, including quality and customer service. The flip side of the coin for deciding where you'll get your products is how you'll ship it. There are three choices: dropshipping, inventory, and a hybrid of the two.

Dropshipping

If you decide to work with a dropshipping company, you don't have to pay for anything until you make a sale. When customers buy something from you, their order goes straight to your dropshipper, which maintains the inventory, packages the order, and mails it for you the same day. You earn the retail price your customer paid minus the dropshipping cost. This cost is higher than their wholesale price because it costs them more to package and ship a lot of small orders to individual customers than it does to ship bulk to you. Don't try to save these costs by waiting to order from your wholesaler until someone orders from you. With Amazon having gotten everyone accustomed to next-day delivery, your customers aren't going to wait happily for two shipping times (wholesaler to you, you to them).

More info on dropshipping - https://hairbiz.tips/dropshipping.

Inventory

With this model, you buy everything you're going to sell, and you package and ship every order yourself. You'll make more per sale and save yourself the dropshipper's fees, but you also have to do all that work yourself. And you have to do it every day. Your customers don't care that you need to go out of town for a funeral. They still expect you to mail their order within a day or two of when they place it, even if you just went to the Post Office yesterday. Additionally, the up-front cost of buying and storing your inventory can run into four figures.

Hybrid

Unless you're on a really tight budget, I recommend this model. It's the one my most successful clients use. It costs more upfront than pure dropshipping, but maintaining a small inventory of what you expect to be your best-selling products allows you to make more money on them. With the hybrid model, you can offer a wide range of products *and* earn bigger profits on the hottest items. Want to go out of town for a week? No problem, you can switch to 100 percent dropshipping for that week. You won't earn as much while you're soaking up the sun or visiting Granny, but at least you can take a break without cannibalizing your business or getting someone else to run it while you're gone. Trust me, your mom doesn't want to pack your orders!

STEP 2. MARKET RESEARCH

It's easier than ever to do market research, and once you've made your decisions about what you're going to sell (the kind of product) and where you're going to get it (the type of supplier), you need to put your chapter 3 skills to work and educate yourself about both.

STEP 2.A. PRODUCT RESEARCH

Having decided on the product(s) you plan to sell, you need to research all the top sites in your niche. Google makes it easy to both find and rank them. The sites that show up in the first few pages of a Google search are almost always the ones that are performing best and selling the most. Go to each of them and look at how they're marketing their products. Get curious.

Use the observation and analysis skills you picked up in chapter 2 and write down what you notice. How are products like the ones you're going to be selling priced? Does the site offer free shipping on everything or only on orders over a certain amount or not at all? Do the sites that offer free shipping have higher prices for their products? (Free shipping isn't free; it's just marketing. The consumer is paying for it, whether it shows up on a line item or is built into the product pricing—I'll explain pricing next.)

Take notes! This kind of market research is valuable on a couple of fronts. One is the intuitive sense you'll get of what the market is like and what your future competitors are doing. The other is hard data: How many products do the most successful sites offer? How are they organized and presented? Are there add-on or impulse purchases made available to shoppers? What kind? How are they displayed? How is the site organized? Is it easy to find what you're looking for? Do you get a good feeling from the site, or is something about it off-putting? Do you stay on some sites longer than others? *How'd they do that?*

Pricing

Your goal is to find a "happy medium" price for your products. I've seen many new entrepreneurs set their prices super low on the theory that everyone's looking for bargains and, to a certain extent, that's true. But people also have internalized the old saying, "You get what you pay for." Price your products too low, and people will assume they're lower quality or wonder what's wrong with them. Think for a minute about your own purchasing decisions. Use something like skincare products as a close example. Do you always buy the cheapest ones? Do you feel better about things you spend a little bit more on?

On the other hand, you don't want to price yourself out. You're an unknown quantity in the marketplace, not Gucci or Louis Vuitton. A crazy high price point, without that kind of brand recognition and prestige, isn't going to work for you.

As you zero in on pricing that's competitive but not cheap, also remember that you want to leave room in your prices to offer discounts, send out coupons and have sales. If you leave yourself only the thinnest possible profit margin, you've got no place to go, and people love a sale!

Remember to take your expenses into your accounting. If you pay X for your product and sell it for Y, your profit isn't Y minus X. It's Y minus (X + the price of the box you ship it in + the cost to host and maintain a website + how much you spend on advertising and marketing + the price of keeping the lights on + a whole bunch of other things). Make sure you know what all those numbers are and how much you're actually making on each sale. In the beginning, your start-up costs are high, so you may not even make your money back. That's okay. Profitability is a goal. So is breaking even. What's critical is that you're moving in the right direction—that you're losing less and less on each sale until you start making more and more. This is why it's so important to know what your numbers are. If you don't know where you started, you can't tell whether you're going where you want to get.

For more budgeting information, see: https://hairbiz.tips/budget.

PRO TIP: FREE SHIPPING

I strongly recommend offering free shipping over a given price point. You'll almost always make the cost you're eating back in the extra products people buy to reach the threshold but remember to figure that into your pricing as well.

STEP 2.B. SUPPLIER RESEARCH

Your decision (Step 1.b) about using dropshipping or maintaining inventory and shipping yourself may change after you do your supplier research. Private Label Extensions has the only dropshipping app on Shopify for the hair business (Dropship Beauty) and the largest hair business community on Facebook. I'm going to talk about what we offer and how we work, but it's much more important to me (remember my *why*) that you start and run a successful company than that you use my site or my products. Do your own research!

Most of our clients use the hybrid model I described in Step 1.b, although we have plenty of people who don't stock anything and are still making a ton of money. For them, it's worth it to take a smaller percentage of each sale as profit in order to spend all their time on growing their company. Packing and mailing orders is easy compared to marketing, but marketing is where entrepreneurs build their brands, find their customers, and increase their sales. Sometimes, as these shop owners get bigger and make more money, they'll switch over to maintaining and shipping some of their own inventory, but many choose not to and just keep their focus on building their relationships with their customers instead. (The key is to understand you have to focus all your time getting customers first.)

If you're planning to go this route, make sure you research different dropshippers. Research the services they offer, the quality and range of their products, the technology they use, the community they've created for their clients (if any), and how responsive they are to customer input.

Five Questions to Ask About Dropshippers

- Do you get the feeling they're dedicated to your success?
- When they pack and ship their products to customers, is the presentation attractive? Can you include a thank-you card? Do they offer custom packaging?
- Will your customers get their orders delivered in generic mailers, or are you able to add your own logo and branding to your orders so that they know what they bought came from your company? (Does the dropshipping company take photos or video of every order shipped to help with any questions about what your customer receives?)
- Do they offer options beyond the basic packaging so that you can do something more elaborate that adds a more luxurious feel, even if the product itself is the same? If they do offer custom packaging, do they have support services to help you design your own?
- Do they regularly roll out new products and services to support their clients?

In addition to this kind of general information you'll want to have about any company to which you're entrusting such a big part of your future company's success, there are two things you should be on your guard against.

Warning 1

Dropshipping companies are difficult to run, and it's entirely too common to see them operate for a while and then dissolve. This can mean your entire supply chain can vanish overnight—a disaster actually worth freaking out over—so make sure you carefully vet whichever one you pick. How long have they been in business? Where are they located? How good is their customer service?

(We often get a big influx of new clients for our dropshipping services when other companies fold. This has happened many times over the past five years after finding out why clients switched to us.)

You can find dropshippers on sites like Alibaba and AliExpress and research the ones that look best to you. I always recommend ordering samples from any company you're thinking about working with, but be aware that it's not unusual for unethical companies to send high-quality samples and then, once you've placed a large order, send either poor quality products to the customers you've worked hard to acquire or to simply take your money and disappear. Because most of these companies are located in China, there's not much you can do about it.

Warning 2

As you start doing your research, you'll come across companies that sell vendor lists for a hundred bucks or so. While this seems like it might be a good solution to the problems of Warning 1, don't fall for it! These vendor list companies aren't doing anything but searching Alibaba and Google and scraping up company names. They aren't doing anything to verify the companies' history or quality, and they don't provide any protection against fraud. They don't send people overseas to check on the manufacturing facilities and shipment capabilities, and they don't monitor the quality of their products. I often know a lot of the companies on those lists, and I know from experience (and from traveling to China) how poor the quality of their products can be.

STEP 3. IDENTITY CREATION

If you're a creative person (and you probably are even if you don't think of yourself that way), this is where our work gets fun. We have an entire chapter on branding coming up next, but for right now, it's enough to know that people buy from brands, brands begin with identity, and identity begins with a name. What are you going to call your business?

STEP 3.A. NAME YOUR COMPANY

I'll bet you've been thinking about this since the beginning. You may even already have a name chosen that you've fallen in love with. That's fine, but even if it's just as an exercise, I strongly recommend you think through the recommendations I'm going to make and test your company name against it. Ideas are easy to get attached to, but I promise you, if you let one go, even though it hurts, you'll quickly find another you like just as well.

Keep your new company name a secret until you've finished all of Step 3!

A great company name is easy for customers to remember and spell, and there's something cool or a little bit unusual about it. CurrySimple is cooler than SimpleCurry, for example. I like to start by thinking of all the ideas or words that might be in people's heads when they think about doing a Google search for the kind of products you're going to sell. With CurrySimple, the "curry" part was pretty obvious. It's what I was selling. But when people want to buy a curry sauce, what else is going on in their heads? A lot of them are intimidated by all the ingredients that go into a good curry. They want all the flavors, but they don't want all the work. They want it to be easy—simple.

People buy products to solve problems. Figure out what problem you solve for people and make that promise part of your company's name.

Here's an exercise I really like for finding cool company names: Get a piece of paper and draw a line lengthwise down the middle. On the left side, write down all the products you're going to carry (wigs, lashes, extensions), the categories of those products (hair, beauty), and words for other things associated with what you sell. Write down all the nouns (people, places, things, and ideas) you can think of that relate to your business. Have fun! Look for words that have personality, but not so much personality that nobody would think to google for them. "Falsies" is more fun than "False Eyelashes," but it's still a word people would use when they're searching for your products.

On the right side of your page, write down all the adjectives—all the descriptive and feeling words that are associated with the kind of experience people want to have when they buy your products. I landed at Private Label Extensions because private labels are all about feelings of luxury and quality and exclusivity. Luxury

Extensions, Quality Extensions, and Exclusive Extensions could all have worked okay, but Private Label says all that plus more.

Once you have a list that's at least ten words long on each side, start experimenting with combinations, one from each side of your line. You're looking for something catchy, memorable, and easy to spell. Don't stop at the first combination you like! Keep going. Push yourself. Say your combinations out loud. CurrySimple sounds simple. It's two short words. Private Label Extensions is a lot more letters. It doesn't promise easy, but easy isn't really what people want with extensions. They want sophisticated, and longer words can be more elegant. Plus, they sound good together.

Bundles	Collection
Wig	Boutique
Hair	Shop
Lashes	Slay
Crown	Heaven
Beauty	Couture
Glamour	Seven
Tresses	Company

Company names with two words starting with the same letter or letters can be great (Church's Chicken, Best Buy, American Airlines), but try not to have the last letter of your first word be the same as the first letter of your second word. Private Label Extensions works, Private Table Extensions wouldn't (and not just because it makes less sense). Write the names you like best as URLs, and see how they look. PrivateLabelExtensions is understandable, even Privatelabelextensions works. Privatetableextensions doesn't.

I love the word "boutique," but it's hard to spell—I get it wrong myself half the time. "Niche" isn't that hard to spell, but how the hell do you say it? (Niche Extensions breaks the double letter rule anyway—nicheextensions—see what I mean?) Spelling (like accounting) is one place *not* to get creative. Private Label Xtensions might look cool, but no one will ever find it online and all I've done is introduce confusion. Don't throw in that extra "S" or use a "Z" instead. No Extenssions or Extensionz. Just don't do it. As a business owner, you want to make things easier for your potential customers, not harder. Don't ask them to remember your unique spelling in addition to your name!

Keep going until you have at least three, but ideally, five possible company names you like, then walk away for a little bit. Go do something else. Which of the names on your list do you remember an hour later? Have new ones come to you?

STEP 3.B. BUY YOUR URL

You don't have a company name until you have YourCompanyName.com. I like GoDaddy, but there are plenty of other places where you can register a domain name. GoDaddy offers a lot of add-on services and up-sells. I don't recommend using any of them, but for registering domain names, I think it's the best.

PRO TIP

Many of the companies where you can register domains offer coupons. Google for "GoDaddy" and "Coupon" or whatever other domain registration company you're using and save a few bucks!

Most of these sites will have a simple search bar where you can enter the company name you want to use to see if it's available and what it will cost to register. If you've decided on WonderfulWigs.com, for example, you'll type Wonderfulwigs into the search box. If it's available, you'll see Wonderfulwigs.com and the price. You'll also see Wonderfulwigs.biz, Wonderfulwigs.net, and WonderfulWigs.org as well as things like Wonderful-wigs.com, Wonderfulwigsbuy.com, and other variations like that. I'd recommend against using any but the .com extension, but some of the other suggestions may be okay if your top pick is unavailable or expensive. Try the other names on your list. If you can't buy your company's name as a URL, you haven't named your company. Find another name.

Expect to pay anything from fifteen dollars to as much as you're willing to spend to buy your company's name as a domain, but remember, this is going to be a recurring expense. If you pay two grand for WonderfulWigs.com, you're going to have to do it again next year. (Technically, you should only have to pay the registration fee, which is around fifteen dollars per year.)

Once you've found a reasonable price on a .com URL for a business name you like, don't buy it!

First, make sure it's also available as a business account on Instagram, Facebook, Twitter, YouTube, and any other social media sites you plan on using. I once saw a big-name model with a huge Twitter following announce she was launching a new line of lashes. She tweeted the name out to over a million people, and she hadn't registered it on Twitter yet! I grabbed it for her before anyone else could, and DM'd her about it. I didn't want anything from her; I was just looking out for a fellow entrepreneur, but you might not get so lucky. People have paid stupid amounts to buy their own company names from people who thought it'd be funny (or profitable) to register them on some social media site first.

Once you have a company name that's available as a URL and on social media, buy the domain and sign up for a business account on Facebook, Instagram, and YouTube. Congratulations! Now you have a corporate identity!

STEP 3.C. GET A PROFESSIONAL EMAIL ADDRESS

If you order something from Target online, you're not going to get an order confirmation email from Target@Gmail.com. Once you have your business's domain name, get an email address that has that name after the @, which will make your business look more professional and legitimate and give your customers more confidence in your organization.

Getting a professional email address isn't difficult, but it's another thing that will initiate a recurring expense—this one monthly. Use it as motivation to keep moving quickly through the steps in the rest of the book!

I recommend using Google's Workspace because you're probably already accustomed to Gmail and because it's easy to set up. If you registered your domain name through GoDaddy, you'll see a button that says "Connect to Google." Once you're there, signing up for a workspace account is easy. Google can verify the domain belongs to you and do all the back-end work to set up your new email address. You can even have it forwarded to whatever personal email you're already using.

I'd suggest setting up two email accounts, Your Name @ Your Company Name.com and Service @ Your Company Name.com. You'll probably need to set up more as your business grows, but those two are all you need to set up communications with vendors and to interact with customers. If you're on a very tight budget and can only afford one, get the Service@ address first.

Once you've bought your URL, registered your social media accounts, and set up your workspace account, you can tell the world your new company's name!

yourname@gmail.com

contact@yourname.com

STEP 4. BUSINESS CREATION

Creating an identity is a great first step, but it doesn't make your business a business. You have to create your company as a legal entity. To be a real business that's able to buy and sell products, hire people, pay taxes, and take credit card orders, you need to register as a *limited liability corporation* (LLC), get an *employer identification number* (EIN) and a business license, and set up a bank account, a

PayPal account, and a business credit card. Don't let this intimidate you! And don't pay anyone to do it for you. You don't need Legal Zoom or a third-party service. I'll take you through each step.

STEP 4.A. REGISTER AN LLC

It's never been easier to register an LLC*, and most states let you do it without even having to go into a state office. Google "Secretary of State" and the name of the state you live in. Make sure the URL you click on has a .gov extension. On the front page of your state's Secretary of State's website, you'll find a link called something like "register an LLC" or "set up an LLC." Clicking on that will take you to a form. Fill it out, submit it, and ta-da! That's it. It will take a few days or a week before you hear back from them either by email or actual letter, but then, congratulations! You're a legally registered limited liability corporation.

*Establishing your business as an LLC (rather than as a sole proprietorship or other entity) is a quick, easy way to legally separate yourself from your business, but I'm not an accountant or a lawyer (and don't even play one on TV).

STEP 4.B. GET AN EIN

You can get an EIN (Employer Identification Number) directly from the IRS. Do not waste money on a third-party service here either. Google "IRS" and "EIN," but make sure the link you follow takes you to a URL that starts with www.IRS.gov. You can do the whole thing online. It takes five minutes, and it's free.

STEP 4.C. GET A BUSINESS LICENSE

Not all states require home-based businesses selling online to have a license, but if you're planning to be a success (and you are, aren't you?), you'll need a license eventually. Besides, having one can't create any problems, and not having one certainly can. Better to protect yourself.

You registered your LLC with the state and got your EIN from the federal government, but cities issue business licenses. Google the name of your city and "get a business license." Most cities will let you do the whole thing online, and it shouldn't cost much while you're still small and not bringing in much in sales.

STEP 4.D. GET A BUSINESS BANK ACCOUNT

This will be one of the first business relationships you establish, so put some thought into the bank you use. I recommend choosing one of the larger banks that has a local branch close to you. You'll need to go into your bank, so convenience is important. Your first thought might be your small local credit union and state-wide bank, but they aren't going to be able to help you if you're traveling overseas—or even across the country—and get into trouble.

Set up your business account with a deposit from your personal bank account, and then make sure you keep those accounts separate. You'll thank yourself later, I promise. For the first two years, expect the flow of money to go only one way: from your personal account to your business account.

Your business checking account should come with a debit card. Use it for every purchase you make that's related to your business. If you run out of money in your business account, don't make a business purchase on your personal card. Move the money into your business account first.

Be smart about every dollar you spend on this account. Now is not the time to start expensing business lunches. Your business isn't making money yet. If you buy a successful entrepreneur a coffee to pick their brain about your business, sure, pay for it with your business account, but remember every dollar you spend from this account is a dollar you're not spending on advertising, and advertising is where customers (and their dollars) come from.

STEP 4.E. GET A BUSINESS PAYPAL ACCOUNT

Some of your future customers will only buy from you if they can use PayPal, but that's not the only—or even the best—reason to get an account set up with them. PayPal also allows you to pay vendors. It charges a percentage, but I think it's worth it if you're buying something from overseas, for the consumer protections it offers.

STEP 4.F. GET A BUSINESS CREDIT CARD

Credit cards aren't free money. Don't get a credit card if you're going to spend more on it than you would on your business debit card. But if you're disciplined and pay it off each month from your business checking account, credit cards can offer the next best thing to free money—points! I'm a points junkie. I buy everything I can on credit cards that give me points toward airline miles.

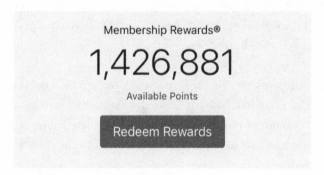

The same rules apply for your business credit card as they do for your debit card. Be frugal and use it only for business expenses.

Get my business credit card and rewards tips: https://hairbiz.tips/credit.

STEP 4.G. GET AN ACCOUNTANT

This is the step everybody skips. Don't skip it! Like getting a business license, there's no way it can hurt to have one, but not having one can actually kill your company. The bank where you have your business account and your accountant are two business relationships that are so critical to your success that you want to start building them as soon as you can.

When you're first starting out, you probably won't need monthly bookkeeping. Once a quarter is plenty. Having someone else to manage that for you is a huge relief, and the hours you don't spend balancing your books can be spent working on your business. Accountants usually cost less than people expect, and between the tax savings they can find and the mistakes they don't make, they practically pay for themselves. There are also accountants who specialize in partnering with small businesses to offer part-time CFO advice and help with common entrepreneurial decisions and calculations, and you can certainly hire one of those if you'd like the extra support.

STEP 5. BUDGET REVISION

In the Your Turn section of chapter 1, I asked you to write down how much you realistically expected to spend on your initial investment and on your business every month. It's time to turn those numbers into a budget.

If you're paying $15 a year for your domain name, that's $1.50 a month. How about your G Suite? What other recurring charges can you see coming? Before you go any further, make sure your current financial position can support your monthly expenses for the non-negotiables: your domain name, your professional email address, and your eCommerce platform (in this case, Shopify).

Monthly Budget

100% Necessity

Domain Name ($15 Yearly)
Professional Email ($5)
Shopify Basic Plan ($30)

Set Up After All Free Options

Email Marketing ($25)
SMS Marketing ($50)
Facebook/IG Retargeted Ads ($150)
Hire Influencers ($100)
Product Giveaway on Social ($50)
Branding Materials ($50)
Samples ($100)

In Step 2 of this chapter, if you did the market research I suggested, you already have a list of possible suppliers. You know how much they charge for various dropship and wholesale options, and you have some idea of how you're going to price your products and what your profit margins look like. Looking at your initial investment and remembering that marketing is the only way to find customers, how much can you budget for inventory?

Don't let your optimism make your budgeting decisions.

Knowing how much money is coming in and going out and how much you can afford to spend on inventory and marketing is very often the difference between success and failure in the first two years. Make a budget. Follow your budget. Keep track of your budget.

Every penny counts. Even—especially—when sales start coming in. It's incredibly exciting when money first begins to trickle into your business account, but don't let that excitement make you stupid. You can maybe ease up a little on how much of your own money you're transferring into the business account, but continue spending what's there only on business expenses. Save whatever you're not spending to build a safety net. Remember, for at least the first two years, all the money in your business account should be spent on or saved for your business. Don't start spending it on yourself—not to pay yourself for your work or to pay yourself back for your initial investment.

STEP 6. INVENTORY ORDERING

Because you did your product planning in Step 1 before you started the money clock, Step 6 won't take long to execute. First, contact the top one or two vendors from your list and order samples to verify they have good customer service and high-quality products.

CAUTION

Be very careful about how you send money overseas. Vendors may recommend using Western Union or doing a wire transfer from your bank, but I'd caution you against this. Using your credit card or PayPal provides some protection against dishonesty and error. I think it's worth the slight additional percentage you may have to pay to have some chance of getting your money back if things go sideways.

Once you have products on the way, start writing the descriptions of them for your website (which you'll build in the next chapter, but which you will have had to at least think about in picking your business name). You'll have a basic description from the vendor, and you will have read up about what you've ordered (or are planning to order), but how you talk on your website is part of your brand. Write your product descriptions with some spice and flair. Write them so people reading them never forget they're reading *your* site, not just some generic one. You want to get creative (but not too creative!) in how you write everything that goes on your website all the way down to the details of each product you carry. I know you don't have a website yet (we'll do that in chapter 7), but trust me—writing creative, fun product descriptions isn't something you want to do for hours in a day. Set yourself a goal of writing one or two a day every day starting now and do it consistently. I promise, in the future, you will be grateful!

YOUR TURN: GET GOING!

Now that you've read through all the steps in this chapter, it's time for you to get into action. Hopefully, you've been taking your turn at the end of each chapter up to now. If you have, you're already prepared. You know why you're putting yourself through all this.

You'll have clear goals and realistic expectations, and you'll have made a solid plan. This is where you put that plan into action.

Get out your notebook and your calendar. Create a to-do list and schedule appointments with yourself to do each of the following steps:

PRODUCT PLANNING

Decide what you're going to sell and how you're going to deliver it. (4–6 hours)

MARKET RESEARCH

Discover what the top sites in your product category are and how they price their products. Decide on your pricing. Write it down! (6–8 hours)

Discover who the best vendors are and write down their terms, shipping times, and customer support information. (6–8 hours)

IDENTITY CREATION

Come up with several great names for your business that are easy to remember and spell and pick one that you can register as a domain name (URL) and on all the major social media platforms. (2–3 hours)

> The money clock starts here!

Buy your URL and register your name on social media and get a professional email address. (1 hour)

BUSINESS CREATION

Register your business as an LLC with your state. (1 hour)

Get an EIN. (1/2 hour)

Get a business license. (1/2 hour + 1-5 days wait time)

Get a business bank account, PayPal account, and credit card. (3 hours)

BUDGET REVISION

Update your budget to reflect the new numbers you now have. (2 hours)

INVENTORY ORDERING

Place sample orders with your top two or three prospective vendors. (2 hours)

NOW YOU'RE GOING STRONG!

Congratulations! You've gone from thinking about starting a business to starting the money clock. You're prepared. You've trained your mind to think like an entrepreneur—to ask *how,* to observe and analyze, do research, and keep notes. You've developed the habit of being consistent (you are still writing those blog posts, aren't you?) and have a personal board of directors for support and feedback. You've learned how you learn and how to handle fear, and you've built habits to help you be professional, manage your energy, and stay organized.

You've gotten going. You've gone from getting it to doing it.

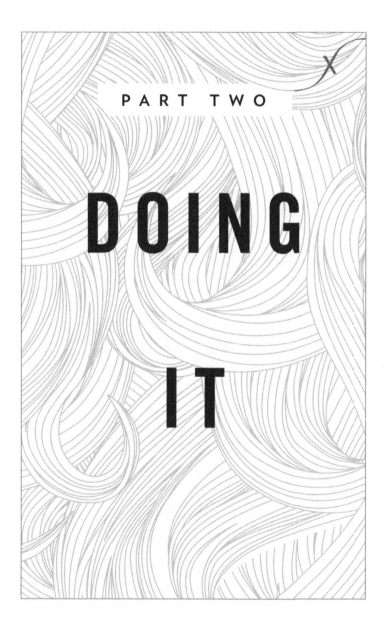

PART TWO

DOING

IT

CHAPTER 5

BRANDING

Think about three of the biggest brands out there: Apple, Target, and MAC Cosmetics. What comes to mind? If I asked you to list five words for each of them, I'd bet that none of the words on your list come from their advertising. They'd probably be descriptive words like "clean," "smart," and "high-quality." I'm making two points here. First, company brands are like human personalities. Secondly, that personality is conveyed visually. Yes, you need words in your ads and on your website, but what you say about your company isn't going to shape your brand nearly as much as the font you write them in. Think about it. If the guy at the bar tells you he works out every day, and he's skinny as your cocktail straw, you're going to believe what you can see, not what he tells you, right?

LET'S DEFINE BRAND

People like to buy from brands. It's how they feel they know something about the organization they're giving their money to. Nobody wants generic hair! People want a brand that they can identify with or aspire to.

Think about the car you drive or the car you'd drive if you could afford to drive any car you wanted to. Would you pick a Ford or a Lamborghini? Why? Each of those brands says something different, and you'll probably pick the one that sounds like you want to be seen. Think how weird it would be for a person to have both a Volvo and a Maserati. If I tell you my friend is a Levis kind of guy or a Louboutin woman, you know something more about them, don't you, than if I said he wears jeans, and she wears heels?

> Brand is your company's personality.

People can be incredibly loyal to brands. It's why, if you order a Coke at a place that carries only Pepsi products, they'll ask you if the substitution is okay. It isn't for some people. If someone would rather drink water than Pepsi (or wear a scarf rather than someone else's brand of hair), branding is why.

It's also why we can talk about Coke having been around for decades, even though no one who founded the company is still alive, much less working there. Brands create continuity.

WHAT BRANDS DO

Most people have a good relationship with Apple's brand (and some have a fanatical one). When the company releases a new iPhone, people line up outside the store for the privilege of giving Apple their money. They don't necessarily even care if the latest model is significantly better than the one in their pocket. It's new. It's from Apple. They want to have it. Some of this is about Apple's "personality." The people waiting outside the store identify with its techy, smart, hip image. Part of it is about trust. People know that if they have an issue with anything they buy from Apple, they can take it to the—wait for it—*genius bar* (genius=techy and smart; bar=hip) and that Apple and its geniuses will take care of them. They trust the brand.

BRANDS BUILD TRUST

You need to create a brand people will want to buy from. Think about what you look for when you shop online. You probably want to feel like you can trust the company with your credit card info. Your brand needs to look trustworthy. That means professional. So should you make your brand look and feel like the version of you that would show up to ask for a bank loan?

Nope. Your brand needs more personality than that, or people won't recognize it when they see it again.

It can be difficult to get this balance right. Much of what looks trustworthy looks bland, and a lot of what gives a brand personality can make it look unprofessional. Try to create an image for your brand that straddles that line, that looks like the version of yourself that would show up if someone asked you to pick up their kid sister from the airport and entertain her for a couple of hours. Trustworthy but fun. Trustworthy and…

Are you going to take the kid hiking? That's trustworthy and sporty.

Are you going to take the kid shopping? You want something trustworthy and stylish.

Brands build trust in two ways: through excellent customer service and through consistent communication. We've already talked about the importance of consistency in chapter 2, but if you look back, you can see we were also talking about brand. If you're slow responding to an email or if you forget to post on social media for a while, it's not you that your customers get frustrated with or forget about. It's your brand. Big companies go to extraordinary lengths to protect their brands. Little companies can't be any different.

Not many people think about customer service when they think about branding. They think about logos and maybe color schemes—the visual components of your brand *are* important, and we'll talk about them in a minute—but anything that affects how your customers feel about your company is part of your brand.

Airlines make the best test for this. If you have a favorite airline— if you'd choose one brand of plane travel over another—I'd bet customer service is the reason. An airplane is an airplane. In fact, most airlines buy their planes from one of only two manufacturers. The only thing that really distinguishes one airline from the other is how they treat you.

How quickly and how professionally you respond to customer emails, how clear your message is on your website, how you handle a situation when something goes wrong—these things directly impact how customers feel about your brand. Remember, brand is like personality. No matter how gorgeous you are, if you don't treat people well, no one will like you.

PRO TIP

A brand is like a personality; not everyone is going to love yours. That's fine. Not everyone likes Apple, Target, or MAC. Don't take it personally.

BRANDS BUILD RECOGNITION

If a customer has a great experience with your hair but can't remember your name, you're not going to make it as a business. Your brand has to be memorable. If you're top of mind when they go to buy hair, they're going to at least come check out what you're selling. The first hair brand I launched was called Luxury Hair Direct. It had all the right components of a good name, but it wasn't memorable and didn't really catch on. Two years later, in 2016, when we launched the brand Private Label Extensions, we had a name everyone loved saying. It sounded exclusive *and* it screamed quality, and it made a huge difference in our success.

Here again, brands are like people. Think about what it takes for you to recognize someone on sight. They need to look at least a little bit different from anyone else, they need to look mostly the same as the last time you saw them, and you need to have seen them more than once. This is what it takes to build brand recognition. We've already talked about being visual. The rest is about being consistent. (Sound familiar?)

You want your brand to look the same everywhere it shows up, and you want it to show up a lot. You need to consistently use the same fonts, the same colors, and the same logo. And you need to stay in front of your customers. People generally buy hair about every six weeks. If someone sees your amazing ad today and wants to try your brand but just bought hair last week, you're not going to make that sale. Five weeks later, are they going to remember they wanted to give your brand a try? If they do, will they remember your company's name? How hard will they try to find you? To stay in front of potential customers, you have to show up consistently. We'll talk about how you do that in the chapter on marketing (chapter 7).

BUILD YOUR BRAND

People are very visual. They'll remember an image before they'll remember a word, so it's important to make your brand visual. You're in control of everything your customers see when they're on your website, and consistency pays off here, too!

YOUR WEBSITE THEME

You won't build your website until the next chapter, but the theme (template) is such an enormous piece of how it looks that it's a major consideration in building your brand. Most platforms have a collection of free templates (more on platforms in the next chapter), but I highly recommend paying for one. For under $200, you can get a template that's incredibly robust and highly customizable and comes with additional features you won't be able to get with a free one.

Shopify has its own store for templates, so if you're using Shopify, you can simply click on the "theme settings" button. If you're using WordPress or one of the other platforms, ThemeForest.net is (at present) the most popular place to find a good template for your website's basic design.

Themes are usually organized by industry or category, and going to the beauty category is a great place to start, but check out other categories if you don't find something that works well for you. You'll be able to change the colors and fonts easily (and you'll have to change the pictures and words) so what you're looking for is something that matches your brand's personality and has the components you want in the places you need them. Think about the theme like the architecture of a house. You can paint the walls, but you can't move the toilet into the living room and expect it to work. Find a template that has the toilet where you want it, but don't pay for it until you've read the next section.

YOUR LOGO

If your company's brand is its personality, its logo is its face. The logo is your company's primary visual symbol. It will go on everything, and ideally, people will think of your company's name the minute they see it, the way Nike pops into your head when you see that swoosh or how the golden arches make you think McDonald's. Nike's swoosh feels sporty. The golden arches are a warm, welcoming yellow. Apple's logo is simple and elegant—smart. It's sleek and modern, like technology. But with that bite taken out of it, it's a little bit subversive—a little bit hip.

Evolution of the Brand

A good logo is clean and looks the same in its tiny Instagram profile picture as it does printed on a T-shirt. (Don't start printing T-shirts!) Logo design is one of the early places you might consider hiring a professional, but you can do it yourself and get good results with a simple graphics program. I recommend Canva.com because it's easier to use than a professional graphic design software like Photoshop—and it's free! Between free and the thousands of dollars a branding company would charge, freelance markets like Fiverr can get you a professionally designed logo for under one hundred dollars, or for ninety-nine dollars, you can get one optimized for the hair industry from PrivateLabelBranding.com.

Logos tend to fall into two categories: text- and graphics-based. IBM's logo is just those three letters in a font made of horizontal lines. The FedEx logo is just those words in purple and orange, and 7-11's is the number 7, with eleven spelled out.

Apple, Starbucks, and Target, on the other hand, use that bite-taken apple, a weird green, two-tailed mermaid, and, well, a target. You don't need a word to know what those companies are. Most companies, however, use a combination of text and graphics. Pizza Hut puts its name (and its restaurants) under a red roof. YouTube's logo is its name with the second word inside a red TV screen.

In 2016, when we rebranded as Private Label Extensions, I worked up our logo in Canva, and it was fine. Later, I paid a designer to remake it. It cost, and I thought it would kill me! But it was a real upgrade and game-changer for us.

More logo tips: https://hairbiz.tips/logos.

YOUR COLOR SCHEME AND TYPEFACES

The Starbucks mermaid is never purple. The McDonald's arches are always golden. FedEx's logo is just its name if it isn't in purple and orange—its colors *are* its brand, and IBM's brand is its typeface. Whatever color or colors you use in your logo need to be the colors of your brand. McDonald's website is red and yellow. Starbucks' website uses the same green of its mermaid. If you consistently use the same color in the same shade everywhere, even if people just scroll by on Instagram, they'll register your color (and by extension, your company) even if they don't stop to look at your post.

Pick colors and fonts that are a good match for the personality of your brand. You want at least two of each and not more than six colors. If you're not good at knowing what colors look good together, you can google "color wheel" and use that to help you. If you're looking for a new font or just something more artistic than what's available in Microsoft Word, Canva.com can help here, too. It's always where I go first when I'm looking for a new font.

If you picked a theme for your website that came with pre-set colors and/or specific or non-standard fonts, be sure that the biggest or most used ones are incorporated into your brand. If the dominant color on the website theme you want to use clashes with the color you want for your logo, pick a new theme. Changing colors and fonts inside a theme isn't always difficult, and the better-developed ones will have a selection box that lets you do so without knowing any code, but it's best to get all that sorted out now.

PRO TIP: WHAT NOT TO DO

Even though you're a beauty company, don't go super-girly (unless you plan to only sell extensions to kids). Pinks and purples are fine, but I'd recommend staying away from pastels, and if you use a girly color palette, pick a more serious font. People are serious about their hair, and even when they're doing something playful or fun with it, they want the company they shop with to take it seriously. Don't use a font that's very abstract or difficult to read, and don't use Comic Sans; it's the bubble gum snapping of typefaces.

YOUR VOICE

What does your brand sound like? How does it talk? If it were a person, would it use slang or perfect grammar? Would it sound excited or cool, like a party of twenty or two best friends talking over brunch? Is it friendly or elegant, down-to-earth, or wildly ambitious? Everything you write for your company needs to sound like your brand. Consistency matters! Decide, as part of your branding, how your company talks, and write your product descriptions, your social media, your website, and your customer service emails all in the same voice.

YOUR ABOUT PAGE

You'll build your website in chapter 6, but as you design your brand, think about how your content will reflect it. In most places, your brand has to hint about who it is. Its personality shows up in the colors you pick, the name you've chosen, and the voice you use. On your About page, you get to just come out and say it. You'd be surprised how many people go to this page—tell people who you are!

Take an hour and put your curiosity and research skills to work. Google, "How to make a great About page." Flip back in your notebook, find the websites you looked at before, and go back and read their About page.

I always recommend to my entrepreneurs group that they make a video to put here. In that video, you can talk about yourself—the person behind the brand. People love this kind of behind-the-scenes inside story, and they feel better about making a purchase from a real person, someone they "know."

In your About page video, talk about who you are, why you

started the company, and what the core of your business is. Keep it short! A minute is plenty of time to get all that across if you've thought about what you're going to say ahead of time.

And please do think about it ahead of time! I promise all the big company's About videos are carefully scripted. Yours doesn't have to be, but the more professional it is, the better. If you know someone with high-quality camera equipment, see if you can borrow it for an afternoon. Better yet, see if they'll come film you. Shoot your video in a well-lit room and make sure what's behind you that will also be on-screen isn't distracting (or embarrassing).

Sound quality is crucial! People will watch poor video quality with great sound, but they'll click right off if it sounds bad, no matter how good it looks. Use an external microphone. The camera on your iPhone is fine—better than even a good video camera from ten years ago—but don't use your phone's built-in mic! You can get away with a twenty-five dollar lapel mic that connects to your phone, but if you're going to invest in making videos, audio is the right place to start.

If you're not going to have a video on your About page, at least have a good, professional photo of yourself. Not a selfie! If you're on a budget, a well-lit iPhone photo is fine as long as the background is professional, and someone else takes it. Obviously, you want to be looking your best for this. Pick out what you're going to wear and do your make-up.* Plan to spend an hour with the person who's taking the photo.

*Any time you wear your own products, you become a walking advertisement for them (unless you're someone like me. I'd just look weird.) Certainly, your picture on your About page and other pictures of you on your site are great places to model your products!

YOUR TURN: BRANDING

DESIGN YOUR LOGO

Whether you opt for text only, image only, or text-and-image combo, make sure your logo looks like your brand and that it's recognizable as a small icon. Keep it simple.

BUILD YOUR ABOUT PAGE

Even if you don't have the video or a good photo yet, make a mock-up of your About page, making sure it includes every element of branding we talked about. Write about the company, its history, its values, and what it offers customers. If you're the face of the brand, you can include some of your personal story here, too. It will help site visitors feel like they have a human connection with you.

CHECK YOUR WORK

Here's a handy branding checklist. It's something you might want to bookmark or add to your notebook to use as a reference while you're building your website, designing your ads, or doing anything else public-facing that represents your brand.

Branding Checklist:

- Personality—does it feel unique and recognizable as yours?
- Trustworthy—will people feel okay about giving their credit card info to your company?
- Recognizable—if people see your Instagram feed later, will they recognize it as yours?
- Does it include a great logo that matches your company's brand?
- Does the writing on the page sound right for your company's brand?

GET FEEDBACK

Print out your About page and give it to several friends. Ask them the brand questions from the checklist. Make whatever changes you need to now before you have business cards, an entire website, and months of social media posts to adjust.

PRO TIP

Be careful of false validation, the tendency of people to shield those they love from uncomfortable truths. Tell your test subjects your feelings won't be hurt, and that honest feedback is actually more helpful right now than praise. Tough love is hard to find but can be the best feedback!

YOUR BRAND

Your brand is your company's personality. It's how people know (and remember) who you are, so it's very important to get it right. But getting it right doesn't mean it won't change. (Google "Apple logo history" and you'll see what I mean!) Your brand will evolve, but it's worth taking the time to get as close as you can to the ideal at the beginning.

And now that your business has a personality, it's time to make it a home.

CHAPTER 6

E-COMMERCE

There's a subset of new entrepreneurs who'll tell you that you don't need a website; you can sell everything through social media. They're wrong. Your website is much more than the place you sell your products. It's your business's home. Private Label Extensions has two (soon to be five) storefronts, but for most hair companies, their first and only location is online.

Think of it this way—where you live on the web is where you live, your URL is your address, and you want to own your own home. If your business's only location is on some other company's social media platform, you're going to be completely dependent not just on that company and its continued popularity but on its technology. The apps, integrations, and marketing hacks that are going to lift you above your competition aren't available on social media sites. And not having a website simply looks bad. A company without one won't seem like a real company to your customers. They'll be less likely to trust you, and they'll have to look harder to find you.

> There's a reason all successful businesses have websites.

I can pretty much promise that any company whose name you can think of has a website. It may be the only thing all successful businesses have in common. And they're not just doing it because it's what everyone is doing. It's because they know it's what they have to do to be successful.

WEBSITES ARE THE HUB

A website will function as the hub of your company. It's a central place that all your social media leads to and where any outside links land. Having your own website lets you do things you couldn't otherwise (like customer tracking), and it's how you become findable on Google.

Your website will also function as a directory of everything your company is doing. It's all your products and all your social media in one place. And if you do open a brick-and-mortar location someday, your website will drive traffic to your storefront. A simple addition to your site will allow you to identify online shoppers who are located close to your physical store and show them a pop-up that invites them to come in and visit. And if they click on the ad, it'll open a Google Map with directions from wherever they are right to your store!

WEBSITES ARE EASY

A lot of people get intimidated by the idea of building a website. They think it's something only computer experts and coders can do. I get it. And it's true, it used to be that way, but it isn't anymore. If you can set up an online account at your bank and post to Instagram, you've got all the technical chops you need. Like most new skills, it'll take a little time to get good at, but once you've gotten the practice, you'll know how to build websites, and how cool is that!

In the last chapter, I talked you through picking out a website template. Building a site really is as easy as swapping out the different elements and modules of the template with your own. Replace the placeholder photos and text with yours; place your logo, and choose your fonts as the defaults. It's truly "plug-n-play," and you'll be shocked how quickly you can have a great-looking custom site that reflects and supports your brand by doing those few things.

WEBSITES NEED A PLATFORM

The software that actually runs the code that makes your website is called a platform, and there are a ton of them available. You've probably seen ads for companies like Wix, Squarespace, GoDaddy, Illusion, Shopify, and WordPress. Shopify is the most widely used platform for e-commerce, and I think it's the best, but you don't have to take my word for it. Shop around, if you want to, but keep a couple critical questions in mind:

- Does the platform support marketing and credit card processing tools?
- Is it well-documented online?
- Does it have good 24/7 customer service?
- Does it offer affordable design themes?
- Can you easily add the apps and plugins that will supercharge your website?

For my money, Shopify not only satisfies all these criteria, but it also has a whole ecosystem of additional features. Because Shopify has made its code easy for software developers to work with, hundreds of them have gone off on their own and developed plug-ins—outside tools, integrations, and functions—that you can have for free, buy, or subscribe to that will let you do pretty much anything you can imagine wanting to do on a website. Some of these are incredibly useful for marketing. (Shopify calls these little additional modules of code "apps," but they aren't like the apps you run on your phone.)

Once you've decided on the platform you're going to use, register an account there. I'd recommend starting with the basic plan and upgrading later if you need to.

Follow the instructions they give you. Most of the bigger platforms have worked very hard to make it very easy for their customers. Shopify, I know, has very simple step-by-step instructions to walk you through how to tie the URL you bought to your account. Design your site first! Once your website goes live, you're in business, so until you're really ready for primetime, keep your site offline. Work on it until it looks and sounds like your brand, has credit card processing and PayPal enabled, and works the way you'd expect any other e-commerce site to work.

> You only get one big debut. Make it count!

WEBSITE DESIGN

Don't get carried away designing your website. Have you ever gone to an e-commerce website to look at the website? I'd bet you haven't (at least not until you started doing market research!). Your customers are just like you are. They aren't coming to your site to look at your beautiful website design. They're coming to look at your products—and hopefully buy them. Don't let your website get in their way. Don't make it hard for them to find your products, don't make them watch an animation before they get to your home page, and don't fill your pages with pop-ups that might distract them from the reason they're there. You want to encourage people to make a purchase and then to make additional add-on purchases—but you don't want to pelt them with calls-to-action.

Be curious, be educated, and get feedback. Once you launch, keep experimenting with different design elements and see how they affect your conversion rate. Continue to observe and analyze other shopping sites you visit, particularly make-up or clothing sites, to see what other companies are doing. Notice the way the ads you see on your social media feeds change. If a website asks for your phone number or email address in return for a new shopper discount, do you give it to them? Does having that discount make you more likely to buy something when you were only planning to browse? Any time anything another website does gets you to click the "Buy" button, document it in your notebook.

RESOURCES

I've had really good luck simply googling for help when I've needed it. If you've noticed you buy more when you have a coupon or add things to your cart to hit a free shipping threshold, try googling, "How to create a coupon on Shopify." You'll get links to articles and video tutorials.

The website BuiltWith.com is also a fantastic resource. It's a little plug-in that runs in your browser, and whenever you go to a new site, it can tell you all the different tools that were used in making it. I've discovered more than a few new, cutting-edge tools this way—in part because I've been looking at websites with that investigator's eye for so long that when something new comes along, I notice it and know it's new. When I spot one, I'll google it to see what it does. If I think it might be useful, I'll run an experiment with it. I discovered the program *In Cart Upsell* this way. It's not cheap ($99 a month), but I decided to give it a month as an experiment, and it made back its purchase price the first day. I would have lost thousands of dollars a year if I hadn't run that single $99 experiment.

APPS

Once upon a time, if there was something specific you wanted your website to do, you needed to hire someone to write that code for you. Today, for 99.9 percent of any functionality you can think of, someone else has already written the code and made it available as an app. Shopify and WordPress (called plugins on WP) both have their own app stores set up to help you find whatever you need. If you're using a more obscure platform, you might need to google to find an app that'll do what you want, but it's probably still already out there.

Apps are amazingly powerful tools, but don't go nuts. Apps slow your website down. Think of them like luggage. The trick is to have exactly the things you need but no more. You don't want to drag around apps you don't need. I know I've clicked off websites that took too long to load. Any additional benefit that merchants might be getting from the app is probably canceled out by lost sales, and plug-ins can't work their magic if they drive all the customers away. A site that's slow to load risks more than losing the impatient among us. It puts its discoverability in danger because Google gives slower sites a lower ranking in its search results.

Get my list of favorite apps and plugins: https://hairbiz.tips/apps.

PICTURES

Like apps, pictures can slow down a website, but they don't have to. You need to optimize and compress every picture you upload. It isn't hard, but it's incredibly important, especially if you're uploading pictures you took yourself. Optimization reduces the file size of your images as much as possible without sacrificing quality, and compression makes it more efficient.

I use PicMonkey for photo optimization—it's free and does a good job, but you can certainly do your own research. For compressing an image, I like compressor.io, which is also free.

PRO TIP

Accurately matching the name to the image and adding the ALT tag makes it easier for Google Search to send people to your website increasing search traffic to your website over time. (More on this later.)

NAVIGATION

Focus your main navigation on product pages grouped by category and subcategory to help your customers get to a product page as quickly as possible, and put the links to things like your legal and terms of service pages in the footer. Nobody wants to click through levels and layers! Again, it's all about making it easy for people to give you their money, and that all happens on the product page level. Besides, it's what they came to your website for and where they want to go.

WEBSITE CORE PAGES

As you build your website, make sure to keep your colors, fonts, and navigation the same from page to page. The template you've chosen will take care of most of this for you if you don't toy around with it too much. It's very confusing for customers if each page of your site feels like an entirely different place!

You're going to need a Home page, an About page, a Contact page, an FAQ page, a blog, legal pages, and product, category, and review pages. I recommend you start with a product page.

The Product and Category Pages

If you followed my recommendation in chapter 4 to start writing product descriptions for a bit every day, you already have many of them written. Congratulations! Aren't you glad you did? If you haven't gotten going on them yet, now's a fine time to start.

I recommend grouping products by category and having an entire page dedicated to each product. If you sell a Brand B lipstick in ten different shades, each shade gets its own page, but only Brand B is listed on the lipstick category page along with lipsticks from Brands A to Z.

It's also a great idea to turn on "breadcrumbs," which display the hierarchy of nested categories. Most templates make this easy to do, customers appreciate it since it makes it easier for them to find what they're looking for and to explore related options, and Google seems to like it, too, so there's really no reason not to go all Hansel-and-Gretel on your site!

The Contact Page

The contents of a contact page are pretty self-explanatory. Put your professional email address here. Either YourName@YourCompanyName.com or Service@YourCompanyName.com.

List a phone number if you can. It's fine if it's your personal cell number (although remember you've done this when you go to answer a call and be sure to change your voicemail message). If you work somewhere that won't let you answer the phone during regular business hours, it's better just not to put a number on the contact page. It will only frustrate your customers to call in the middle of the day and get no response.

If you have a physical location, give the address. If you don't, consider getting a Post Office box. You're going to need a place to accept returns, and publishing your personal home address on the web just isn't a good idea.

Include an email form. People prefer to fill out forms directly on your site when they want to contact you. Having an email form makes it easy for them to reach out without having to click off your site and over into their email program.

Set response expectations. Tell your customers (and potential customers) that you answer every email and return every call, and commit to a timeframe for when they can expect to hear back from you. It shouldn't be any longer than one business day, and if you can commit to a shorter window, do it! But it's much better to under-promise and over-deliver than the other way around. Say you return all messages by the end of the next business day, but tell yourself you'll always do it within six hours.

The Review Page

You should create this page now, but don't take it live or link to it until you have at least eight reviews. Fewer than that, and you're likely to spook customers. Make sure this page allows people to upload pictures of themselves in their new hair, and include the review form that feeds this page on every product page. Customer reviews should appear both on the individual page of the product they're reviewing and on the review page where all customer reviews get aggregated. Oh, and there is an app for that! (Actually, there's a bunch on the Shopify app store; just pick one you like that gets a good rating.)

The Blog Page

Your blog page is a single page that lists all your blog posts and automatically updates its list when you create a new post. If you've been playing along, you should already have a few posts written. This is fantastic! An empty page immediately identifies you as a newbie. When you build your front page, you'll add a feed from this one, too, which will go a long way toward making sure your homepage has regular updates to boost its Google ranking.

The FAQ Page

An FAQ (Frequently Asked Questions) is a great time-saving tool. It dramatically cuts down on the number of emails you have to answer if a customer can get their questions answered here. It also does double-duty as blog content.

Don't make your FAQ too long, and expect to adjust it as actual questions start being asked. Experiment with the questions you post. If you remove one question-and-answer, do you start getting emails with that question, or does nobody seem to miss having the information?

I recommend picking the five to ten subjects that you think are likely to generate the most questions. Shipping, haircare, and returns are obvious choices. Think of the questions that people are most likely to ask and write the answers in a short paragraph and add them to your FAQ page.

Legal Pages

You need to create four legal pages: your terms of service, your refund and returns policy, your shipping policy, and your privacy policy page. Don't let this intimidate you. Shopify has a template service (free, whether you use Shopify or not), which provides standard language for all these pages with places for you to enter your company's name to customize them to your site.

Home Page

This will be the first page your customers see, but I recommend doing it last because you don't really know everything that needs to be on it until you've built the rest of the site. Make sure your company name and logo are clearly visible, but don't waste customers' time with a home page that only goes one place. Remember, customers want to get right to the product they came there to buy, and that's what you want, too! List all your product category pages here as well as links to your other core pages and to your social media accounts—we'll talk about those later in this chapter.

GET TO THE TOP OF GOOGLE

As a search engine, Google's job is to direct people to websites based on the terms they search for. How it decides who gets sent where has a lot to do with the size and popularity of the site, how close of a match it seems to be for what the user wants, and an insane host of other factors. Google considers the words and images on your website (and your competition's), the number of people who've visited, how long they stayed, and what they looked at when it decides who shows up where on the list of search results it shows the person who searched. You want to get on the first page, (no one scrolls to the second page of search results) and SEO is how you get there.

SEO

SEO stands for Search Engine Optimization, and it refers to anything you do to make your company more visible to Google. Because it's by far the largest and most widely used search engine, pretty much anyone who finds your website by searching for it finds it through Google. Obviously, it's well worth your time to tip the scales in your direction, and you can get about 80 percent of everything SEO can do for you in just 20 percent of the time by concentrating on content, keywords, and tags.

Google Analytics tracking software and the Google Search Console are free to use and provide site owners with the same extraordinary amount of information it uses to decide who shows up at the top of the search results list. I recommend setting up both of them and adding an item to your list of recurring tasks to check in with them weekly. Don't expect a lot to monitor at first, but they'll prove increasingly useful the longer you're in business.

PRO TIP: DON'T PANIC!

About once a quarter, Google launches a new update, which makes it look like the world has stopped coming to your site. Don't let this freak you out. If you see a sudden drop in your site traffic, google to find out if Google just released an update. If they have, give your numbers a week or two before you make any major decisions based on them.

Get my top SEO tips: https://hairbiz.tips/seo.

Content

The first and most important thing you can do to improve SEO is to make sure the content of all your blog articles and social media posts are centered around the same things your business is. Keeping the focus on hair in your company's social media feeds, in the articles you write for your blog, and in the videos you post to YouTube does more than support your brand and make you look professional. It increases your ranking with Google.

Google knows how many pages people visited and whether they scrolled down the page. Do everything you can to make the experience of visiting your site a good one. Write blog posts people want to read all the way to the end. Make your site visually interesting but easy on the eyes. Encourage visitors to browse around. Use engaging images and videos. People who wouldn't stop to read four paragraphs will often stick around to watch a video, and they're more likely to stay with it until it's over than they are to read a blog post or a product page all the way to the end.

Keywords and Tags

Keywords are the words people use when they search, and you want the highest density of them that you can get. When you upload pictures and videos, you have the opportunity to enter a few words of description. Make sure these words are keywords! This lets you get double duty out of all your marketing messages and turns even informational and educational posts into sales posts.

I've cautioned you in a few places about not going in for the hard sell. You don't want to be yelling at people to buy stuff all the time, but when you post a detailed tutorial with step-by-step instructions about how to color extensions, for example, SEO tags let you build more than goodwill. Also, people will watch a video longer or read more of something that doesn't feel like an ad, and if they're doing it on your site, the longer they stay, the better it is for your SEO.

The basic package of your platform will offer some free SEO tools—use them! The most common and useful of these tools is the Alt tag which gives you the ability to invisibly attach a description or keywords (called metadata) to an image file. To get the most out of this, add photos to your site that can show up when people do an image search and take advantage of the metadata.

Title and meta tags both describe a webpage, with the title tag coming first and the meta tag containing more information. I know adding a title and meta tag to every page on your site sounds like a lot of work, and it does add to the time it takes to set up a page, but it pays off! It's what Google shows your potential customers. What you put in the title tag provides that bolded first line in the search results, and the information you put in a meta tag is what Google uses to give people an idea about what they'll see if they click on the link, but it's actually a form of free advertising. Try to make it interesting and attention-grabbing so people will click on your link rather than the one above it.

Of course, you can just pay Google to move you up in their rankings, but I don't recommend doing so at first. There's a more profitable advertising investment you can make—Facebook.

FACEBOOK IS YOUR FRIEND

I strongly recommend investing serious time on your company's Facebook page. Repost your blog articles here and work hard to create a community around your brand. This is easy to do—in fact, Facebook probably encourages you to start a Facebook group for your business every time you log into your site's profile. These groups are a great way to interact one-on-one with your customers and to collect valuable feedback. Start posting now if you haven't already to build some pre-launch buzz for your business.

PRO TIP

Keep your personal and business Facebook accounts separate. Your friends will get tired of hearing about your business, and your customers don't want to see your dog.

Facebook Pixel

Facebook collects an insane number of data points about everyone who uses it, and this can be incredibly good for you. As you start to build an audience, Facebook will know what music they like, what movies they go see, whether they have kids, how much money they make, and a lot more. Having this information allows you to create incredibly targeted ads to reach the people most likely to buy your products, and it keeps us all from seeing lots of ads for something we have no interest in. Facebook Pixel is a little string of code you add to your website, which increases the amount of information you have about the people who visit, allows you to follow them when they leave, and connects directly to your Shopify account. It's also the only right way to advertise on Facebook and Instagram.

PAYMENT

The final function your website needs is the ability to accept payment. No matter what your larger *why*, making money is part of the picture. If you're using Shopify, this is almost trivially easy. Simply install Shopify Payments, which is built into the platform, and set up the backend to transfer money to your business checking account. Shopify will handle all the credit card processing for you.

I strongly recommend giving customers the additional option of using PayPal for all the same reasons I mentioned in chapter 4. PayPal provides both you and your customers some level of protection against fraud and, more importantly, some people simply won't (or can't) make credit card purchases. You'll lose their business if you can't offer them an option. Don't however, use other payment systems like Cash App or Venmo. These are a great way for informal services, but you're a professional now and your business needs payment systems that are scalable and which can automatically create orders in your shipping system and make your accounting easier.

Learn more about payment processing: https://hairbiz.tips/payments.

YOUR TURN: E-COMMERCE

Choose the platform you're going to use, set up an account, and connect your URL, although don't set it to "live" or publish anything to the world yet.

Create your product and category pages first. Keep their design simple, easy to navigate, and in line with your brand. Install the plug-ins (apps) you need, and be sure to optimize and compress all image files.

Build your core pages: an About page, a Contact page, an FAQ page, a Reviews page, legal pages, and a blog.

Create your home page—the face of your company in the world. Make sure it makes a great impression!

Optimize your site for Google—it's how people will find you.

Install Facebook Pixel. It's the best tool out there for marketing on social media.

Get feedback on your website.

Before you go live with your company's site, have a friend or two test it out to make sure it's as clear and easy to use as you think it is.

Build your social media presence by regularly posting to Facebook and Instagram.

Start publishing blog posts on your website and link—promote— them to your company's Facebook page to generate excitement about your grand opening.

OPEN FOR BUSINESS!

Don't take this step before you're ready, but once you're ready, do not hesitate. Once your website is online, discoverable through Google, and linked to social media, congratulations, you're in business!

SCHEDULE RECURRING E-COMMERCE TASKS

Being in business comes with new opportunities to flex your consistency muscle.

Weekly

1. Monitor your web traffic. How many people are going to your website? Is that number increasing (on average) each week? Are they finding you through Google's search results or following a link from one of your social media accounts?
2. Monitor your conversion rate. What percentage of the people who arrive at your site end up making a purchase?
3. Publish a new blog post of at least a thousand words, with pictures and a minimum of two external links and five internal links to things like product pages or other blog posts on related topics. Post a link to it from all your social media accounts.
4. Make a new video and post it to all your social media accounts.

Daily

1. At least once a day, check your business email account and respond to every single message.
2. Monitor your social media feeds and respond to any comments or direct messages.

YOUR WEBSITE

Congratulations, you have a website. You're officially in business! But you're still missing one crucial element—customers.

CHAPTER 7

MARKETING

In May 2020, I held a Sunday sales event. It was an experiment. I thought it would be fun and hoped it'd be profitable—I set a goal of $15,000 in sales for the eight-hour event. We did $36,000. It was amazing, but it was chaos!

The next month, we responded to the feedback from that event—both the overwhelming positivity from our customers and the positive overwhelm of our staff. We didn't do much marketing for the event that month; we were focused on implementing what we'd learned. We took a step back to look at everything we could improve and made plans for what we needed to organize. The second event did $46,000 in sales and made us confident we'd worked out the kinks.

My sales goal for the third time we held the event was $50,000. We did $97,500. In one day. The only significant difference between the $46,000 event and the $97,500 one a month later was marketing.

THE ROLE OF MARKETING

Once you've opened for business, marketing is your single most important activity. (Remember customer service is part of marketing.) Marketing encompasses everything that you do that affects customers and potential customers. Without it, no matter how carefully sourced and high-quality your products or how beautiful your website, you don't have a business. It's not a party if nobody comes.

Most entrepreneurs struggle with marketing at first. It's going to take time for you, too, to learn to do it well. There isn't a formula or an exact science behind what works and what doesn't (or what works today and doesn't tomorrow). It's a trial-and-error process that never stops. My big Sunday sales event was an experiment that worked, but I've certainly had some that didn't! You will, too. Don't get frustrated. This is where the consistency superpower you've been developing really pays off.

> Successful marketing is the difference between business success and failure.

THE GOAL OF MARKETING

Marketing introduces people to your brand, turns them into customers, and keeps them coming back. I like to think about it like dating (and not in the "I have a girlfriend and haven't done it in a while" way!). "Dating" means a lot of different things to different people, and I don't mean to imply anything or exclude anyone when I use my experience as a man interested in women as an analogy for marketing—it's just the scenario I know best (and I promise not to talk about tapping the market!)

When you first launch your business, it's like moving to a new city.

You don't know anyone, and nobody knows you. Sure, you might have some friends and family, but, as I mentioned in chapter 1, new entrepreneurs are frequently surprised by how little overlap there is between their people and their customers. You can't be looking to your friends and family for sales (or dates!). You have to get out there and meet people.*

*Our analogy breaks down a little bit here since you're looking for hundreds and eventually thousands of new dates, which doesn't match my experience, but think about introducing yourself to customers as dating at scale.

For your company, "getting out there" means posting on social media and all the free advertising you can do (specifics coming up) because at first, your only goal is to build some name and brand recognition. When people first land on your website, they know nothing about you. Your business is just something that was recommended by someone they follow on social media. Making a great first impression is crucial! This is the moment where you introduce yourself. In our dating analogy, you say hello, and the girl says, "I've heard of you." Whatever she's heard, all it's done is buy you permission to make that first point of contact, to say hello—but not much more than that.

This is why you put so much time and attention into designing the main page of your website—it's your date outfit. You need to look good! You want to be interesting. If she's on your site, something she heard or saw made her curious enough to click on a link. She's made eye contact with you, and you've said hello. She may not be looking for a date at that exact moment. That's fine. Make a good impression, and maybe she'll remember you when her interest in dating changes. Not everyone who comes to your site needs hair right then, but if they like what they see, when they are ready to buy hair again, they won't have already ruled you out. This is another place where consistency matters. She won't remember you or know where to find you two months later. You need to keep putting yourself out there, so you're around for her to see you again and come back to your site when she's ready to make a purchase. Think of it as going to the same coffee shop as she does in the hopes of bumping into her.

MAKE A GREAT FIRST IMPRESSION

Everything we talked about in website design is part of this. It's your clothes and hair and your opening line. If the customer is actually in the market for hair right then, it's how easily they can find what they're looking for. It's why you've made it very simple to get to product pages.

Your goal is to "date" every customer who comes to your store so you want to get their phone number or email address so you can show them more ads, but you don't want to come on too strong or ask for too much too quickly. The quick one-time purchase is great, but you're looking for a long-term relationship, and that takes time. Push too hard for the sale today, and you might ruin your chances. Customers want to be wooed, to learn more about you, to trust your brand, and to feel good about the transaction.

BE CONSISTENT

In the same way you want to keep showing up in people's social media feeds, you want to keep making a good impression. Every interaction a customer has with you needs to be positive. If she comments on a post, don't ignore her! Reply promptly to every comment and email.

Once someone makes a purchase and becomes a customer, don't take them for granted. I recommend hand-written thank you notes for every purchase when your company is still new enough and small enough for that to be practical. Pay more attention to and take better care of your customers than potential customers. It's tempting to get sucked into an "I need more customers. I need more customers!" mindset—and it's true, you do—but make sure you're always targeting your previous customers and trying to turn them into repeat buyers. Then turn those repeat customers into fans. It costs much less to invest in keeping a customer than acquiring a new one, and fans that talk up your products and brand can actually bring new customers in.

ADVERTISING SUPPORTS MARKETING

I've already said that marketing is everything you do that faces your customers—from the design of your website to the quality of your products, from how quickly and professionally you handle customer service to how you package orders. Advertising is the subset of that "everything" that's the most obvious about its agenda, and it, in turn, breaks down into two sub-agendas or advertising goals: drive traffic and increase conversions. Two types of ads accomplish this: prospecting and retargeting.

To return to our dating analogy, prospecting is the "putting yourself out there" kind of advertising. It's everything you do to get a first date, and retargeting is everything you do to get subsequent ones—to have a person who's visited your site come back. Conversion is the advertising word for "converting" a prospect—someone who's seen you on social media and visited your website—to a buying customer—someone who actually purchases your product, the first step in building a relationship with you (and here, we should drop our dating analogy.)

TERMS OF THE TRADE

Traffic—The people who come to your site.

Conversion—Traffic converts when the people who come to your site buy something.

Conversion Rate—Your conversion rate is the percentage of traffic that converts—the ratio of the total number of people who come to your site to the number who make a purchase. If half the people who come to your site buy something, you have a conversion rate of 50 percent (and should open your own ad agency!—the average conversion rate for new businesses is 1 percent. In other words, you should expect to get one sale for every hundred people you bring to your site.)

We'll go into detail about different kinds of ads in a minute, but Mikey's First Rule of Advertising applies to them all.

Mikey's First Rule of Advertising: Free First!

Your budget is limited. It's especially limited when you're first starting out, but even Coke, with $4 billion a year (that's over $7,000 a minute 24/7/365) to spend on advertising, has a ceiling. Since, in your first year, you're likely to have less to spend in a year than Coke does in an hour, you need to use every dollar wisely and get the most out of every free option.

A lot of what I've already been talking about as part of building your brand is also free advertising. Posting on social media, creating a YouTube channel, and writing a blog are all ways of getting your company in front of people that cost you nothing. Take full advantage of them!

ADVERTISING'S CORE SKILLS

Like everything else worth doing, advertising takes practice, and practice takes time, which means you'll move slowly and do badly at first, but you'll get both better and faster as long as you stick with it. There are a tremendous number of options for advertising—different channels and techniques—and you'll need to experiment with some and figure out others. Don't get frustrated or discouraged! Be prepared for it to take a while.

Advertising is a process of trial and error, the proverbial spaghetti-throwing enterprise, and in the beginning, you're going to hurl a lot of pasta, and not much will stick for a whole host of reasons. But as your brand evolves and your company grows, you'll start seeing incremental improvements, month after month, and year after year.

TERMS OF THE TRADE

"Call to action" is an advertising term for things like "Buy now!" and "Check it out!" It's any message that tells people to do something—to take an action. Learning to craft calls to action that influence people to take actual action is a terrific skill to have! So is making sure to include one in all your ads and marketing messages. In the hair business, there are only a few actions you want customers to take: visit the site, sign up for a newsletter or text list, or (best of all!) make a purchase.

AUDIENCE SELECTION

The next chapter is all about building and maintaining your relationship with your customers, but a subsection of that belongs in advertising because the better you know your audience, the more effective your advertising will be. Part of this is because you'll know what they want, but part of it is because Facebook lets you tell it which audiences to show your ads to. (More about this in the next section.)

PRO TIP: WHAT NOT TO DO

Don't pay to boost posts. They're not advertising for you; they're income for Facebook. You might as well make a cash donation.

Don't spend money on Google. Do all the free stuff you can to improve your ranking, but don't pay to move up the list or run ads. There are entire books about how to use Google Ads, and maybe in a few years, you'll want to read a couple and start educating yourself on how to get your money's worth. (Or maybe you'll hire someone to do it for you.)

USING FACEBOOK

When you're starting out in the beauty industry, Facebook ads are the serious power players and the only advertising worth paying for. (Facebook owns Instagram, so when I say "Facebook," I mean both Facebook and Instagram.)

You set up your company's business account on Facebook back in chapter 4, and you've been doing all the free stuff: posting to your page, responding to comments, cross-posting from your blog. Now, assuming you have money budgeted, it's time to start buying advertising.

Go into the Facebook Ads Manager and click around a little. When you're familiar with its interface, start going through the steps of deciding the demographics you're targeting. There are categories for age, location, gender, race, and income level, and there are options for different interests. Facebook does a great job of matching the audience you specified with the people who are most likely to buy something from you.

Of course, Facebook does this because it's in their best interest for your advertising to lead to sales because then you'll buy more Facebook ads. In the same way you want to sell high-quality hair, so your customers come back and buy more, Facebook wants to sell high-quality ads. Advertising is Facebook's product.

Start with a budget of five dollars a day for each ad. Even if you can easily afford to do so, it's not smart to spend more at first. Facebook's algorithm needs time to figure out how to get you the best value for your money, so you're better off not spending as much until it figures it out. When one of your ads leads to a sale, spend a little more on it—a little more. As your business grows, slowly dial up what you're spending in five-dollar increments because, somewhere, there's a wall beyond which more dollars don't equal more sales. You don't want to spend those dollars.

Using Facebook Pixel

In chapter 2, I called Pixel the most powerful marketing tool available, and in chapter 6, I explained how it fits into your larger e-commerce marketing strategy. In the section below, you'll see how it works its magic when I rank the four types of campaigns you'll run most frequently from least to most effective. The top three all rely on Pixel.

The Facebook Pixel tracks every single thing every visitor does on your site. It records every page they visit, every product they click on, what they put into their shopping cart, and whether they made a purchase or left before doing so. If they enter their shipping address, it knows that. It knows *everything*. All this information goes into building a profile of each site visitor, which allows you to deliver the most effective ads directly to the people most likely to make a purchase. Pretty great, right?

If you've been taking Your Turn, doing the activities and recommendations of this book, you will already have Pixel installed. If you don't, do it now! Do it before your website goes live. Every person who sees your site is an opportunity lost without it.

RUNNING CAMPAIGNS

In advertising, a campaign is like a battle inside a larger war. You might run several different campaigns at the same time, all of them advertising your company, but each focused on doing a different thing like introducing people to your company, advertising a sale, or launching a new product.

Broadly speaking, the campaigns you'll run most fall into one of four types. Ranked from least effective to most, they are: prospecting, general retargeting, product catalog, and abandoned cart ads. You'll start by running only the first and add new ones when you hit certain targets until you're running all four.

Facebook typically lets you run six different ads within a single campaign. It runs all of them equally at first, then it figures out which ones are the most effective and shows them more frequently.

Types of Campaigns
Prospecting

Prospecting ads earn the least for every dollar you spend on them, but they're the first kind you have to run. (I know, it doesn't seem fair, does it?) You run these ads to introduce your company to the wide world of people who've never heard of you. All these ads can do is drive traffic to your site, but it's the only way to find potential customers for your business and get that traffic ball rolling.

General Retargeting

When your website is averaging around a hundred visitors a day, you can introduce the second type of campaign. General retargeting ads are shown only to people who've already been to your site. (See why we can't do them first?) They have a higher conversion rate than prospecting ads, but they're still mostly for familiarizing people who came to your site to read a blog post or watch a tutorial video with your brand.

Product Catalog

Once you've doubled your traffic again and are getting an average of two hundred visitors a day, you can add an even more effective ad. Facebook lets you import your entire catalog of products into their system to create product retargeting ads. You know you've experienced this kind of advertising if you've ever been looking around a website, maybe checking out different ways of keeping your feet warm in the wintertime, and then later, when you were on Facebook, you started seeing ads for wooly socks and tights.

These ads are so effective because they're so targeted. They're only being shown to people who you know are in the market and actively looking to buy something you'd like to sell them. Your ad reminds them of that, and many times, they'll click back and buy it.

Abandoned Cart

The conversion rate on these ads is amazing! They're by far the best return on your advertising dollars, but only if you have enough people coming to your site to make them worthwhile. Let your traffic go up by a hundred again to three hundred visitors a day before you pull the trigger on abandoned cart ads. What these ads do is probably pretty obvious from their name. When someone puts something in the shopping cart on your site and leaves it there, these ads remind them. Most of the time, people actually meant to hit the "Buy" button, but something interrupted them, or their wallet wasn't nearby.

CREATING ADS

Now you get to be creative! What your ads say and look like is entirely up to you, and you should have fun experimenting, but there are four best principles to keep in mind and three different elements you can consider using.

BEST PRINCIPLES

Make your ads consistent with your brand. Ads are usually the first point of contact you have with potential customers, so you really do get two chances to make a first impression—the first time a visitor arrives at your site (which we've already talked about) and the first time they see one of your ads. Your ads need to look and sound the way your brand does.

Make your ads inviting. You know your customers better than anyone (you do, don't you?), so design your ads to appeal to what they like and what's likely to make them curious enough to click the link and go to your site.

Make your ads easy to understand. Keep your designs simple enough that people know what they're looking at and understand what you're saying to them.

Include a call to action!

THREE ELEMENTS

This is going to sound really obvious, but it's important. You have three ways of getting information to people: words, pictures, and videos. If this sounds familiar, it's because it aligns with the different learning styles we talked about in chapter 3, which is why you want to use all three in your ad (but not necessarily all three in every ad.) There are some people who will never, ever click on a video and others who won't read text, but pretty much everyone looks at pictures.

Image Ads

There are a lot of software options for doing graphic design, but I like Canva.com for this, too. Image ads are great for prospecting. You can show pictures of your products or a model wearing your hair, but you can also use images that support your brand. Just remember to follow the principles above and don't try to put too many words and images in a single ad.

Retargeting Ads

Catalog ads don't take a lot of design work on your part because Facebook basically builds them for you using your products. All you need to do is load your product catalog into its ad manager and let it do its thing. General retargeted ads might point to a blog post or informational article about the products. You don't always have to be selling. The abandoned cart retargeted ads should add a sense of urgency and mention the customer "forgot something" by not completing the purchase.

Video Ads

You can make video ads yourself, use a video production company, or hire an influencer to make them for you. When you're first starting out, you'll probably do all of it yourself, and that's fine. The same basic principles from above still apply, and so do the guidelines I gave you for making an About page video: Keep it short, plan what you're going to say, and have good sound quality.

Your video ads really don't have to be highly produced. In fact, ads shot with your iPhone can end up looking more natural and relatable than something really highly produced. A video that goes viral is like winning the web traffic lottery. It can be huge! But you can't really plan for it to happen. It's a dream more than a goal. Make great videos that have that potential and hope, but don't count on it happening or be disappointed when it doesn't.

> Let me tell you more about Facebook marketing: https://hairbiz. tips/facebook.

WORKING WITH INFLUENCERS

An influencer is anyone with a large social media following, and the larger the following, the more influential they are. Micro-influencers are people with under 10,000 followers, and it goes from there all the way up to people with over 100 million, and you can pay them to promote your company.

This is one of those rare places where bigger isn't always better. The larger an influencer's following, the less targeted it is (and the more it will cost). There are plenty of micro-influencers out there with small but really dedicated audiences who watch and listen to everything they do and are more likely to try out something they see there.

I highly recommend the website BeautyClout.com if you're looking for influencers to promote your beauty products. It lets you search by different categories and interests, shows you the profiles of influencers in those categories, and you can ask for bids on how much they'll charge to promote your product or hire them instantly for a set price. Some of the smaller influencers don't even charge; they just want free products in exchange for their review.

Don't do this right away. Wait until you've already spent some time building up your website, collecting reviews, and refining Facebook's algorithm because this is a place where retargeting really nails it. Most of the people who come to your site from an influencer won't stay long at all. They'll click over, see what it's all about, and leave. But if you've got the Facebook Pixel up and running, you can start sending them those lovely, highly effective retargeting ads that are much more likely to lead to a sale.

OTHER MARKETING TECHNIQUES

There are a few simple things you can do to increase sales and boost your brand that technically fall outside the realm of advertising but are well worth your time to set up and use: reviews, rewards, giveaways, referrals, sales, and up-sells. Do the four types of advertising I've given you above first, but experiment with some of these techniques, too.

REVIEWS

I mentioned reviews in chapter 6 when we talked about setting up a review page as part of your core website, but I didn't explain much about why it's so important to have a place to collect reviews and to collect them in the first place. Getting (good) reviews is probably the most impactful thing you can do to drive sales short of paid advertising. Reviews generate sales, but you can't really work on getting reviews until you're already getting sales. Luckily, once people have started buying your products, getting them to write reviews for you is pretty simple.

Follow up with every person who's bought something from you about two weeks after the sale and ask them to leave a review on your site. At first, you'll do this yourself, but once you're getting several sales a week, you can upgrade your email program to do it for you automatically. Most people don't mind writing reviews, but you are asking them to do something for you, so it's a great idea to offer them something in return. For some reason (and I really don't know what it is), coupons aren't a good answer for this. Offering a customer a coupon to write a review feels almost like you're spamming them. Offering them reward points, on the other hand, feels great, although it's basically the same thing.

Jenny Smith

I really loved the body wave bundles. Once installed they were soft and bouncy. I got so many compliments at work. I am in love with this company!!!

REWARD POINTS

People love to collect things, and they really love to collect things that save them money. There are several different programs that can integrate with your website to help you set up and manage a system of giving customers points for purchases, reviews, and referrals. (It's another thing Shopify makes easy.) I think it's something well worth doing because people love rewards almost as much as they love free stuff.

GIVEAWAYS

Question: Why would a company ever give away anything for free?

Answer: It doesn't.

Companies do giveaways to promote new products, to drive traffic to their site, and to create an incentive for doing something that benefits the company. When you offer a giveaway that directs people to your site, when they go, you get the chance to use retargeting to bring them back to buy more things later. Giveaways can be a great way to encourage people to leave a comment or follow you on social media.

Question: Why would a company ever give away anything for free?

Answer: Because they want to give back to the community.

At Private Label Extensions, we regularly give free wigs to cancer patients, and we support Black entrepreneurs by giving away hundreds of free websites and design products, and about fifty laptops a year to help people run their businesses. I believe in good karma, supporting those that support us, and overall just be good to people. It will pay dividends in life.

REFERRAL SYSTEMS

Word-of-mouth is the most effective marketing there is. It's what you're buying when you pay an influencer to promote your products, but even someone they admire isn't as persuasive to your potential customers as someone they know. After someone makes a purchase, you can offer them something like ten dollars off their next purchase if they recommend your site to a friend and that friend makes a purchase.

SALES

Everybody loves a sale! They're easy to set up on Shopify, but make sure you promote the heck out of any sale you run. It's also a good idea to put a time limit on sales and include that information in your advertising to create a sense of urgency. "Get 20 percent off for the next twenty-four hours or while supplies last" will bring in more traffic than, "Get 25 percent off now." People don't want to miss out on a good deal!

For a few months now, I've run a sale once a month that's called "The Drop." It happens at noon on a Friday, and everything is released and on sale for the next twenty-four hours. People haven't been able to see all the products ahead of time, so the sense of urgency is intense. Suddenly, the products are there, and they're on sale, and if you don't get them now, they'll be gone, and for an entire day, it's a feeding frenzy on the site.

We've been around for a while, we have a long mailing list and a huge collection of products, so don't expect the same thing to work the same way for you, but it will work. Once again, there's something like an invisible dial you have to fiddle with. You turn it as you start to grow, trying to match your marketing to your company's size and needs.

To use Private Label Extensions as an example again, the first drop was basically a test run, and we did $16,000 in sales in twenty-four hours. I thought that was pretty good, so the next month, I built on the fact that people already knew about the sale, and I added more products, and we did $32,000 in sales in the same time period. That's double! I kept turning that dial, adding products, retargeting people, and reaching new ones, and the next month we more than doubled our sales again, doing $65,000 in twenty-four hours.

But I can't keep doing the same thing and expect sales to keep doubling. Remember, that dial has a top end. You can't crank it past eleven. An offer loses its sense of urgency if people know it's going to roll around again forever. I'll keep twiddling the dial, watching how results change, looking for what's most effective. You have to keep your finger on the pulse, experiment, and adjust.

UP-SELLS

Up-sells are their own kind of marketing magic. I mentioned them in chapter 3, where I suggested you watch for them in your own shopping experience. When you're looking, you'll see this technique used everywhere—from the candy bars and magazines at the grocery store to, "Would you like fries with that?" Everybody does it because it's incredibly profitable. What's great about our industry is that upselling isn't sleazy. People often genuinely need the products you suggest as add-ons, and sometimes, they wouldn't have known if you didn't tell them. And it's a marketing technique you can use from the get-go if you have the extra one hundred dollars to spend because it can be effective even on your very first customer.

Here's how it works: you install an upsell app for Shopify (or other platform you're using), and you set it up to suggest certain products as an additional purchase when someone adds a particular product to their cart.

My favorite example is with wigs. If someone shopping on your site spends twenty minutes picking out exactly the right wig and puts it in their cart, they may not be thinking of it at the moment, but they're going to need a way to secure that beautiful new wig they're so excited about once it comes in the mail. If you've set up your app, it'll simply ask them if they need wig grips. Or lace glue. Or a way to remove the lace glue, or a way to clean the lace. You don't want to drown a customer in suggestions and pile on everything they'll need one thing after another.

Package deals are a fantastic kind of up-sell. You can give the customer everything they need already pre-selected and packaged for them *and* give them a discount on the wig because you'll make up the difference in the purchase price of all those extras they might not have purchased otherwise.

OTHER SOCIAL MEDIA

There are plenty of social media platforms other than Facebook and Instagram where you can prospect for clients—Snapchat, TikTok, Pinterest, and YouTube. When you're just starting out, it's best to build your presence and following on just one platform before trying to be everywhere to avoid spreading your budget too thinly. Once your Instagram page is attracting a strong and growing audience, you can leverage them to build up your You-Tube channel (for example) by offering them a special deal found only there. Be creative with your strategies, and don't just post the same videos at the same time on every platform. That's boring. Don't be boring.

YOUR TURN: MARKETING

If you've been playing along, you will already be obeying the first law of advertising (free first!). Now it's time to start your advertising career. Keep doing all the free stuff, but start building your first prospecting campaign. Make sure your ads are true to your brand and include your logo and a call to action. Start with a budget of five dollars a day and watch your traffic and sales numbers. Experiment with different images and calls to action and see what works best for your audience.

When your site is averaging one hundred visitors a day, start your first general retargeting ad, but don't stop running your prospecting ads. As your daily visitor numbers increase, you'll add product and abandoned cart ads but also start experimenting with some of the other marketing techniques.

YOUR MARKETING

Marketing is like breathing—as long as your company is alive and wants to stay that way, you need to be doing it. Unlike breathing, there are a thousand different ways to do it, and not all of them work right away. There are techniques that might be incredibly effective for your company in its fifth year that will totally fail in your first. Be careful, experiment, and analyze your results. Marketing is crucial; it's the only way you have to talk to your customers, but you don't want to be that guy either. You also need to listen.

CHAPTER 8

COMMUNICATIONS

Private Label Extensions has the largest Facebook group in the world dedicated to helping people get started in the hair extensions business (Start a Hair Extension Business)—https://hairbiz.tips/group—and here's your official invitation to join us if you haven't already. That Facebook group—in fact, the entire company that supports it—was the direct result of customer communications.

When my buddy told me what his girlfriend was spending on hair, and I decided to get into the hair business, the company I started was its own brand of hair. I started using Facebook to find people who might be interested in selling our brand at their beauty parlors and salons in return for a commission. The response I kept getting wasn't super-enthusiastic about selling my brand but incredibly excited about having a brand of their own. Based on that, I decided to pivot my entire company in 2016. We went into the business of starting brands for other people and supplying hair products to them through dropshipping.

Nearly five years and over $30 million later, I'm still listening to customers and making decisions based on what I hear. Some companies pay consultants a lot of money to do research on what the market wants, but I think you can get just as good, if not better, information just by listening. We've expanded our business, started offering new services, and implemented new technology, all based on what our customers were telling us they needed to make their businesses more successful. I'm incredibly proud of all of it, but my favorite thing is when people think I'm psychic.

It happens all the time. It happened with lashes. It would never have occurred to me on my own to offer a line of lash products, but people were talking about it in the Facebook group. I looked into it, and a couple of months later, we rolled out our lash line. People loved it! They said it was like I'd been reading their minds.

I can't read minds (I don't think I'd even want to; that could get messy!), but I'm deliberately very involved with my customers. I'm proactive in my community. I read what people post, and I take it seriously. If I see enough people asking for the same thing, I do what I can to get it for them. That's about as close as you can get in business to a guarantee of success. If people want a product and I get it for them, they'll probably buy it. They're happy to have it, and I'm happy to do what it takes to have it to sell.

> Listen to your customers!

Listen to your customers on every channel they're using—email, comments on social media posts, their own posts on your Facebook or Reviews page. My company has grown to a team of more than thirty, but it's still me in there on the Facebook group because I want to keep my finger on the pulse of my customers. And we talk about it. My team has a weekly discussion session, and most weeks, we talk about what people are asking for at least part of the time.

I credit a huge portion of the success I've had to how responsive we've been to customer communications. You may not want to go as far as to pivot your whole business around what you hear from your customers, but if you don't listen at all and ignore them, you're not going to keep the ones you have, and new ones are much more expensive to acquire.

Communications isn't the sexy, cutting-edge part of running a business. It's not like sales events and new product rollouts and photo shoots. It's not what you dreamed about doing when you imagined running your own company, but it can make the difference between getting to keep running your company and having to fold up shop.

BRAND YOUR COMMUNICATIONS

Remember, a company's brand is its personality. I'll bet at some point, you interacted with a brand that had a bad attitude. I'll also bet you don't do business with them anymore. If you're not a government agency, your business has competition, and your customers will take their business to them if you're being a brat.

Make "responsive" part of your brand.

I've seen some new hair companies fail because the founder couldn't get out of the nine-to-five mindset they'd picked up in the work world. As an entrepreneur, you're not on the clock—or maybe it's that you're never off it. If it's ten at night and you need to hop on the computer to answer some support tickets before bed, it's worth putting on your CEO hat with your jammies. Your customers will appreciate your help (and they won't know what you're wearing!).

It is incumbent on those intrepid souls who endeavor to shepherd a nascent organization through its inchoate beginning to the very pinnacle of success to meticulously maintain and safeguard representations of identity such that those differentiating attributes maintain a high degree of consistency and fidelity to the original and not to subject one's audience to discordant or baffling variations.

See what I did there? It just feels weird when brands look and sound one way in their ads and on their websites, and then sound like something totally different and boring in their communications with customers. Make sure what you say sounds like you. Your emails should sound like your blog posts, which should sound like your product descriptions—and if you write a book, it should sound like you, too. Don't be a robot!

LEVERAGE YOUR COMMUNICATIONS

Not only will your customers feel like they know your brand and like it better when you communicate well with them, you can also use that communication to ask for something. Let's say you answered that 10 PM email and went back and forth with the customer once or twice, helping them sort something out and making sure they were happy. If you end that conversation with, "Thank you," they'll go away happy. If you end it with, "Hey, you know what? This has been a great conversation. You're such a happy and amazing customer! Would you mind taking just a minute to leave a review here: www.link-to-product-page?" they'll go away happy, *and* they're more than likely to do something that will really help out your business. For bonus points, add something like, "Please reply back here when you're done. I'd love to see it!" It'll increase the odds that they'll remember to write their review.

OUTREACH

You focus all your content and use keyword tags to increase your ranking with Google so that it will send people to you. Outreach is how you go to them. Now is not too soon to start gathering email addresses and phone numbers for email and SMS (text) marketing.

I don't love pop-ups on websites that make visitors give their contact information in order to see beyond the most generic content, and I don't recommend asking for anything right away. Again, it's like dating. You don't ask for a phone number right after you say hello. Spend a little time with your website's visitors before you ask them to give you the okay to email or text them, and don't keep asking every two minutes if they don't enter anything the first time you ask, but SMS and email marketing are simply too effective not to ask at all.

Change It Up

You want to keep putting your company in front of your potential and repeat customers, but you don't want to be that guy who only talks about one thing. Develop marketing messages in different categories and rotate them even if some create less of an obvious and immediate return on your investment. Customers respond differently to different kinds of messaging at different times; the variety pays off eventually, and it keeps you from being that one-note guy.

Applying the eighty/twenty rule, 80 percent of your communication should be informative, educational, or instructional, and only 20 percent used for selling. Don't worry, the 80 percent will still increase your sales, just less directly. People don't always like a hard sell, and following the eighty/twenty rule will keep you from alienating people by pushing too hard and warm up your customer base.

Marketing Messages

Your blog posts and advertising carry a marketing message, too, but here, I'm referring specifically to your SMS and email outreach messages, which come in three categories: sales, information, and education. Here's an example of each:

Sales

We're having a flash sale today on (product category X). Save 20 percent with this coupon now through 9 PM!

Information

Hey guys, we just opened a West Coast shipping facility, so you don't have to live in the eastern half of the country to get your packages the fastest!

Education

Check out this tutorial video where we show you how to color our best-selling extensions and make them look amazing.

Combination

We've launched a new product! Here's a video on how to use it, and hey, because it's something brand new and we want to get it in your hands, here's a limited time discount code for you!

> **PRO TIP: SHOPPERS LOVE COUPONS!**
>
> Most e-commerce platforms have coupon and discount systems built in, which can handle the vast majority of what you'll want them to do, but there are additional, advanced coupon and discount plug-ins you can buy if you want to expand those capabilities.

Email

Email marketing has been around a long time, and it's easy to overlook, but eventually, it will probably drive close to 20 percent of your sales, so it's still a big deal. It's great for general marketing campaigns, just to keep your company at the top of people's minds, but it's also a fantastic way to get useful information to people.

To be successful with email marketing, you need to sign up for a third-party tool. MailChimp is probably the best-known, but sadly, it does not play well with Shopify. I recommend Klaviyo, but several email marketing platforms have started getting smarter recently, so I don't know what will be best in breed by the time you're reading this. Do a little research and pick one.

Marketing emails are a great tool, but don't send too many, and make sure you're only writing them when you have something valuable to say. Don't copy-paste every blog post into an email, but email is a great way to let people know about an upcoming sale or new product you're introducing.

Email also gives you another path for retargeting since you can set up an automatically generated email to go out to customers who stalled out somewhere in the check-out process. Just a quick email saying, "Hey, we noticed you left something behind!" with a clickable link back to their cart can be very effective, especially if you include a discount!

Finally, email is a great tool for marketing-as-customer-service. Your shopping platform will capture email addresses whenever people place an order, and I think it's always a good idea to send a customer service-oriented email about two weeks later. I recommend something like this:

> Thanks so much for your purchase. If you had a great experience shopping with us, we'd love for you to leave us a review here*. If you haven't signed up for our rewards program already, you can do that there, too. If there was something we could have done better, please reply to this email to let us know about it.

*Include the link to the reviews page (which should include information about your rewards program).

Obviously, you want to reword that to sound like you, but the advantage of constructing your sales follow-up email this way is that it funnels your happy, positive customers to the website to leave a review and alerts you of any problems people are having. Most of your customers will have had a good experience, but it's inevitable that not all of them will, and most unhappy customers never let you know about it; they just don't come back. Asking for feedback—positive or negative—shows your customers that you really care about their experience and gives you a chance to get their issues fixed and win them back as customers.

Overlapping with this are specifically targeted customer win-back emails. You can set these up to go out to customers who haven't made a purchase for a couple of months. Don't think of these as marketing emails. They should feel more like a heart-to-heart conversation about whether you did anything that let them down and maybe asking if they've seen some of your cool new products.

Email techniques and services: https://hairbiz.tips/email.

SMS

Text marketing is much newer than email marketing, but it's been proven to be even more effective. Emails can get lost in your inbox, and people have to actually open them to see the message you sent, but when was the last time you got a text you didn't look at?

This is exactly why you want to send texts to your customers very sparingly. Because they almost *have* to look at them, customers will get resentful of your interruptions quickly if you send them too frequently or don't use them to deliver useful information.

Of course, the emails you send should be useful, too, and carry some urgency, however small. People get annoyed by being interrupted for things that don't at least feel time-sensitive. If you're running a sale, especially one that's active for only a short time, send that text! People often appreciate learning about the chance to save some money, but every text you send should have a clear call to action.

You have to be more careful with SMS than with email because the costs can add up quickly. Make sure you're using whatever ad tracking you have available through your platform. Many SMS apps that integrate with Shopify can calculate the ROI for each SMS campaign for you. This is the only way to know where you're getting your money's worth, and where your energy is being wasted. If you spend twenty dollars to send a text that advertises a flash sale and people who click over from that text to your store end up spending , that was twenty bucks well spent. If no one clicks the link or if no one who does buys anything, you might consider putting that money into Facebook ads.

CUSTOMER RELATIONSHIP MANAGEMENT (CRM)

CRM Systems are incredibly powerful, but they aren't cheap, and you don't need to have one right away. When you're first starting out, you'll be able to do it all yourself, and the next step is to add the kind of third-party tool we talked about in the last chapter, but eventually, you're going to want to upgrade. For me, that "eventually" is the moment you feel like your email is starting to feel a little messy or unorganized. Don't wait! The bigger your customer database, the more difficult the transition is going to be, and you've worked too hard to damage your brand with something as avoidable as unanswered emails.

Your CRM system can send out automated emails and track your response times when customers reach out to you. I set goals around lowering my response times—one hour max by 2021—because I think it's so important. Look at it this way: if you were shopping for hair and had a question, and you emailed two different stores, what do you guess the odds are that you'd make your purchase from the company that answers you first? I'd bet they're pretty good.

My CRM recommendations: https://hairbiz.tips/crm.

PRO TIP

Shopify can give you a breakdown of purchases by customer—how many orders any given customer has placed and how much they've spent. This is huge! It lets you identify who your top customers are. Get this information and take very special care of these people.

SPECIAL COMMUNICATIONS

You want to take great care of all your customers, but you want to take even better care of your best customers. Most e-commerce platforms make this easy to do. Shopify includes this information in its dashboard, but you can always simply filter your customer list by how much they've spent on your site and discover who your best customers are that way. Make these people feel special because they are special to your business.

Find ways that are consistent with your brand to develop and deepen your relationship with these folks. I recommend reaching out to them directly, one-to-one, especially early on, where one or two really great customers can have a huge impact on your bottom line.

Consider creating a special email VIP filter for your best customers and use it to send out special deals or "secret" information—like a new product line you haven't launched yet.

Some rewards programs have tiers, with the top one reserved for the really big spenders. Delta Airlines was famous for this kind of system with its top-level Medallion Members getting such great treatment that people bought flights just to level up. Get creative about how you can take special care of your special customers.

YOUR TURN: COMMUNICATIONS

How are you listening to your customers? Experiment with ways to get customers to leave comments and reviews, read what they post to your Facebook group, and look for trends in which of your blog posts and videos get read and shared most.

Look back through your company's sent mail. Does it sound like your brand? If not, make a plan to fix it.

YOUR COMMUNICATIONS

Without customers, you don't have a business. Stay curious about them and educate yourself, but communicate with other entrepreneurs, too. The Young Entrepreneurs Council (YEC) and the Entrepreneurs Organization (EO) are great places to start surrounding yourself with like-minded people. Join local business organizations and groups like ours on Facebook. Finally, I invite you to communicate with me. If you've built your business as you've read this book, I want to know about it! Text me at 404-476-5181.

CONCLUSION

I started working when I was fourteen because I wanted to help my mom. When I started my first business, she was my first why. I truly did not want her to worry anymore. She'd worried all her life, and I just wanted her to be happy. And we got there. Last year, I told her I was planning to pay off her condo and that there were enough frequent flyer miles piled up to fly her anywhere in the world she wanted to go. Turns out, she wanted to go to her high school reunion. I pulled out my phone, logged into my Delta app, and bought her a ticket—first class. She was in her sixties, and she'd never flown first class, but I knew she'd enjoy it. I think it felt better for me to buy it than it felt for her to sit there on the flight to her reunion.

She said she had a good time seeing old friends and hearing everyone brag on their kids. She stayed for two days and got on the plane to come home. First class boards first, so there she was, sitting in her big, comfy seat as people she'd seen at the reunion walked by to their seats in coach. Mom said they all kidded her about it, "Oh, first class, huh?" and she laughed with them, but she felt so special. She was finally, suddenly, the coolest kid in class. I don't know that I've ever had a business success that's made me feel as good. It'd be enough on its own, but I love that it was where she got to sit on the airplane that made her so happy since it was not being able to sit there that had first got me asking the entrepreneurial question.

Even if Mom hadn't died, I would have needed a new *why*, and I think it would have been the same one—to help other women start the kind of company that let me buy my mom that ticket. It took me longer than I wish it had in part because I wasn't prepared. I had a *why*, but I didn't have goals, realistic expectations, or a plan. I hope that now you do.

You're prepared for it to take two years and to move slowly at first. You're prepared for starting your own business to be emotional and to require sacrifice. You know to expect problems and not to count on your friends to be customers. You know already that there will be slow periods and that you'll have to put the company first. You know it will be hard and that you'll have to say no a lot. You're a lot more prepared than I was!

Being prepared for what it's really like to start and run your own company will help you be more successful more quickly, but it's really the skills in the second chapter that will make the biggest difference—defining your why. If you can learn to ask yourself the entrepreneurial *how*, to get curious, make a practice out of observation and analysis, and record what you learn, you'll be way ahead of where I was.

Learning to be consistent internally, to make plans and follow them so you can be consistent in your company's externally facing tasks will give you a superpower that can multiply everything else you do. Learning to seek out, get, and accept feedback—

both positive and critical can save you from making many of the mistakes I made. If you can do all that and then learn how you learn best, you can start to tweak your habits and your behavior to better handle fear, be a professional, manage your energy, and get organized. Then you're ready to go!

I wrote the first half of this book to help people understand the mindset and skills they need to do what they want to do. If you can get the Part 1 Getting It ideas, you can absolutely do the Part 2 "Doing It" tasks. How do I know? Because I did, and if I can, anyone who's willing to put in the work can, too.

Having finished this book, you've taken the first steps. If you're reading this, having done a first read-through, it's time to go back and start taking your turn. If you've been doing that all along, you're already in business. Congratulations!

Either way, it never stops. You'll keep learning, developing new and stronger habits, and experimenting. You'll get great at things that were really hard at first, and you'll run into new things you don't know how to do. Owning your own business means being in the business of problem-solving. The problems never stop. Neither can you, although eventually, you can take a little time off.

Around the two-year mark, you can think about taking a short vacation. If you've been reinvesting in your company as I've suggested, you might not have much money for a vacation, but if you've been making all your business purchases on the right card, you may well have enough points for a flight or hotel. And I promise you, a vacation paid for with points is the best vacation an entrepreneur can have!

At one of our weekly Thursday night dinners together, not too long after her high school reunion trip, Mom mentioned that she'd like to go see her mom. I promised to book her a ticket, and the conversation moved on to something else. After a while, she got quiet. She ate a little bit more, and not looking at me, said, "Can you book it first class?"

I can't promise you'll get to see your *why* come true quite so vividly. I recognized I was very, very fortunate to give my mom that sense of safety she'd been lacking all her life before she died. But I can promise you that if you want to try, I want to help you. You can find online classes, extra resources, and a weekly planner on the book's website and a large and vibrant group of other people engaged in the same work and benefiting from each other's experiences (and frequent prize giveaways) on our Facebook group.

One sale a week can change your life. A sale a day can pay your rent. Starting a business can teach you about yourself and train you to be better. I learned a lot of what I know about how to run a successful business by owning one that failed. I learned what I needed to know the hard way, and I've put it all between these pages. It can't make you fearless, but it's a solid blueprint. If you get the Getting It and do the Doing It, you'll have started your own hair business. You and it are my new *why*. Let's be fearless. It's beautiful.

ACKNOWLEDGMENTS

I am forever thankful for everyone who has been part of the last seven years of this journey:

My girlfriend, Mary Margaret, was there day-in and day-out during the best and worst moments.

Mom, you were my motivation for success. You did everything you could to help make me great. I would give all the success away to bring you back.

Raj! You have been a great business partner. Also, the one I call the luckiest guy in the world. Thanks so much for letting me run with this!

The Start a Hair Business Facebook group! You guys are my tribe, and my dedication to making you successful in the hair industry will never slow down. Love ya!

The amazing team at Private Label Extensions. We did it! I can't thank you enough, Mr. 2.0, Zakiyrah, Tiara, Mary Anne, John

Raymond, Mai Thai, David, and everyone else who has been part of the PLE family for the past seven years.

Yo! Dallas Christopher! You were the first stylist I connected with within the hair industry. Now you are a partner with Private Label. We are just getting started, buddy!

The Scribe team! Skyler, you are the absolute best, and I am so thankful to have worked with you and the rest of the team.

My cats, Sir Minion, Lady Underling, and Lord Butler.

My sister Kerri, and step-brother Dwight for always looking out behind the scenes. And my nieces Sadie and Audrey for energizing me with your young spirit.

Last but not least, my clients. As you know, I can't name names because we are Private Label, but none of this would have been possible without you. I want to thank you from the bottom of my heart. I will continue to provide the best products, services, and knowledge to help you be amazing.

ABOUT THE AUTHOR

MIKEY MORAN is a serial entrepreneur and the founder and CEO of Private Label Extensions, a hair extension and technology company helping entrepreneurs launch and manage their brand, ranked #278 of the *Inc.* 5000 and the #1 fastest-growing beauty business in the country by *Cosmetic Business*. Mikey has been featured on ABC, Fox, CBS, CNBC, *Forbes*, and *Entrepreneur*, among others. He is also the co-host of the podcast, *Hair Biz Radio*, and the founder of the influencer platform, Beauty Clout.

Made in the USA
Coppell, TX
11 December 2021

68085307R00121